Additional
Christmas Moments

Additional
Christmas Moments

*67 Stories Celebrating
the True Spirit of Christmas*

COMPILED AND EDITED BY YVONNE LEHMAN

GRACE
PUBLISHING

BROKEN ARROW, OK

Three Wise Men Photo © Kevron2001 | Dreamstime.com

ADDITIONAL CHRISTMAS MOMENTS
67 Stories Celebrating the True Spirit of Christmas

ISBN-13: 978-1-60495-023-4

From Samaritan's Purse

We so appreciate your donating royalties from the sale of the books *Divine Moments, Christmas Moment, Spoken Moments, Precious Precocious Moments, More Christmas Moments, Stupid Moments* and now, *Additional Christmas Moments* to Samaritan's Purse. What a blessing that you would think of us! Thank you for your willingness to bless others and bring glory to God through your literary talents. Grace and peace to you.

Their Mission Statement

Samaritan's Purse is a nondenominational evangelical Christian organization providing spiritual and physical aid to hurting people around the world.

Since 1970, Samaritan's Purse has helped victims of war, poverty, natural disasters, disease, and famine with the purpose of sharing God' s love through his son, Jesus Christ.

Go and do likewise.
Luke 10:37

You can learn more by visiting their website at www.samaritanspurse.org

Dedication

Dedicated to
Terri Kalfas, who saw the beauty
and value of sharing praise in
Divine Moments
Christmas Moments
Spoken Moments
Precious, Precocious Moments
More Christmas Moments
Stupid Moments
and now makes it possible
for the sharing of
Additional Christmas Moments

and

to all the authors who shared their stories
for this compilation
without compensation
just for the thrill of being useful
and being part of the mission work of
Samaritan's Purse
who receives all the royalties
from the sale of these books.

Contents

Introduction

*A*dditional Christmas Moments is the third compilation of Christmas stories by authors ranging from first time published to multi-published...and even some who claim not to be writers. However, they each have meaningful stories that will inspire, encourage and delight as the true meaning of Christmas emerges.

I used all of my personal stories in the first two books. But I'm pleased to say that my son and grandson have articles in this one. My son, David, tells of his best Christmas as a child, which occurred when he was seven years old. Luke, David's son, shadowed me for 13 hours as part of his high school senior project. He was required to write and speak about the life of a professional writer. I gave him the assignment of writing an article for *Stupid Moments*, which I was compiling at the time. He missed the deadline (understandable... I mean, what teenager ever has a stupid moment!), so he wrote one for *Additional Christmas Moments* about his most memorable Christmas, which, interestingly enough, occurred when he was seven years old.

Because Christmas and family often go together I might as well mention one of my daughters too. I have other family members but will save them for another time. Lori Marett, who has written for the Moments series, teaches the Sunday school class I attend. The class members decided we should have a movie night. Lori had talked about the documentary, *The Star of Bethlehem*.

I said, "We could watch that."

She looked askance. "It's about Christmas."

"Wonderful," I said. "We should celebrate Christmas every day. The real meaning of it, that is."

That settled it. Everyone agreed. They also agreed to meet at my house at 6:00 p.m., April 18, 2016. We ate the finger food they brought. I had told them, like I tell my writers group, "If you want to eat, bring it. I provide water and coffee."

They brought a variety of delicious finger food that made it seem like open house at Christmastime — sandwiches, ham rolls, cocktail sausages, cream puffs, fruit-filled cookies, cappuccino bites, and of course popcorn. I may have forgotten something, but I'm getting fat just thinking about it.

We ate and watched the DVD, about which the following comments are made on the back of the DVD case:

> Scholars debate whether the Star of Bethlehem is a legend created by the early church or a miracle that marked the advent of Christ.

Is it possible that the star was a real, astronomical event?

> From producer Stephen McEveety (*The Passion of the Christ*) comes an amazing documentary on the Star of Bethlehem. This presentation, as seen by tens of thousands in the U.S. and in Europe, explores the exciting truth of Scripture and reveals the evidence for God's existence as seen in the stars above. Presenter Rick Larson walks you through Biblical and historical clues revealing the incredible significance of this celestial event as well as the vastness of God's creativity. Discover the secret of the Star — a secret of magnificent beauty.

> http://www.bethlehemstar.net

> We saw His star in the east and have come to worship him.
> ~ Matthew 2:2

Those of us who have faith don't need scientific proof of things like how such a star could appear. God could have flung a new one out there if he wanted to. But having a scientific explanation brings a new sense of awe and wonder. In Psalm 19 King David tells us the heavens speak of the glory of God and the skies display his marvelous handiwork; they make him known without sound or word, and their message goes to all the world. It's awesome just seeing the creation around us, but even more thrilling to understand more fully the way God had the star appear, why the wise men followed it, found the Christ child, and fell down and worshipped him.

In the second chapter of Matthew, he tells us the wise men were "filled with joy." The authors who contributed to this book exhibit that joy when they sent their stories throughout the year…stories that might be happy or sad, about Santa or Jesus, but all representing Christmas as a celebration of Jesus's birth.

The authors are thinking about Christmas all year long as they write and send their articles. They do not give gold, frankincense, or myrrh. They give of their time and effort and are "filled with joy" to know that any royalties go to Samaritan's Purse, a godly organization that reaches out to the world. The first story is an example of the wonderful spirit of these authors who share their stories. All because God gave to us His Son so anyone who believes in Him will not perish, but have eternal life.

That's something to celebrate all year long!

~ Yvonne Lehman

Operation Christmas Child

Did you ever feel a passion for a ministry? Did you wake up in the morning thinking about it? Did it cross your mind during the day? Did you begin to pray for ways to do something about it?

I hope God gives you that feeling and desire because it's such a blessing to know the Holy Spirit is doing something deep inside.

That is how the Shoebox ministry invaded my life. In 1993, I heard about shoeboxes filled with small toys and hygiene items going to Bosnia where a civil war raged. There was a need to reach out to children whose parents had lost their lives. Small children were alone, wandering the streets and digging through trash dumps desperate to find food just to survive.

I began working with the shoeboxes and now lead that ministry in my church. How fulfilling to know that in the name of Jesus 100-million shoeboxes have been delivered to hurting, needy orphans and destitute families in desolate areas.

The people who pack shoeboxes are encouraged to write notes to a child and express that Jesus loves them and gives hope for a future in heaven through their trusting in Jesus to forgive their sins.

The recipients of the shoeboxes can sign up for a discipleship class. After graduation, they receive a New Testament Bible in their own language. Children who had little hope of graduating from school are proud to have a certificate of completing the 12-week class, learning about Jesus, who loves them.

The flying shoebox logo is known all over the world, from refugee camps to mountains tops were people have fled from war-ravaged cities. These people have fled with only clothes they're wearing and a few household items.

Imagine receiving a brightly wrapped shoebox from someone you never knew and with the hope of heaven in it. These contain tooth brushes, soap, washcloths, pictures, books, cards, fun games, stuffed toys, balls, crayons, coloring books, pencils, erasers, small calculators, sewing kits, t-shirts, socks…and on and on. Oh, and of course, hard candy.

Wow! What a Christmas, whether it's December or July!

For over 20 years, working with the shoeboxes has been the best part of my Christmases. This year, in addition to the church ministry, I plan to pack 25 boxes, one in the name of each member of our immediate family. I will send them a thank you card from a child in need.

My desire is to meet these children in heaven and have one tell me, "I got your box." Can you think of anything as rewarding as that? A living soul — saved for eternity — because you and I sent the gospel of Jesus Christ via a shoebox.

Every January, I start thinking about all that has to be done, and it comes together by November. During those months, I remind myself to be faithful. Jesus takes care of the rest.

Jeremiah wrote in Lamentations 3:22-23 (NLT): The unfailing love of the LORD never ends! By his mercies we have been kept from complete destruction. Great is his faithfulness; his mercies begin afresh each day.

~ June Schmidt

Do You Hear What I Hear?

In 1976, during our first Christmas in rural South Carolina, nine-year-old Frankie would test the legend of animals speaking at midnight on Christmas Eve.

"Mama, you promised," Frankie kept reminding me. "You said we could try to hear the animals speak tonight. I've been good. I've been real good all year. I did all my chores, feeding the pony and cleaning out his stall. I gave food and water to Molly. I fed the chickens and gathered the eggs, even when they pecked me."

Trying to discourage him from his midnight vigil, I warned, "It's cold. It's going to be in the thirties. You won't be warm enough out there. And don't forget how dark it is. You can't have a light on, or the animals won't speak."

"I've got my sleeping bag. It will be okay." It was settled in his mind that he would stay with the animals and hear them wish Jesus a Happy Birthday at midnight.

At 11:30, bundled in his flannel pajamas and robe, Frankie was ready to start the 100-foot trek to the barn. In the dark. With only Molly, his dog, by his side.

"Trigger won't bother about me. He knows I'm a kid. If you're out there he might not talk. I wonder how the chickens will sound?" Frankie yawned. Back straight, pillow under his arm, he marched out the door.

I sat on the porch watching shadows sway as if the trees were raising their branches in praise. A forlorn train whistle sounded in the distance. 11:45.

My mother's heart said a quiet prayer. "Lord, I know it's just a fable. But you said that all of creation would bow down and worship you. Even the rocks would shout hosannas. Please, wrap my son in your presence, give him comfort in this vigil. Soothe his mind when the animals don't speak."

Because, of course, animals don't talk.

I heard the whirring of the spring as the clock chimes began to toll.

One. Two. Three.

What was happening in the barn? Seven. Eight. Nine.

The chickens began to murmur as if disturbed from their sleep. Ten. Eleven.

Trigger added his voice as he knickered loudly, covering the last sound of the chimes.

"Happy Birthday Jesus." I heard, followed by Frankie's laughter. Molly joined the chorus. Her joyful bays pierced the night.

Turning on the flashlight, I ran towards the barn.

"Mama, did you hear them?" Frankie asked, excited. "I was very quiet. Then, I could understand the chickens talking. The rooster didn't want the others to talk, because I was there. Trigger told them it was okay because I wanted to wish Jesus a happy birthday too." His face glowed with wonder. "So all together, while the clock was gonging, we sang Happy Birthday. And then I hollered, 'Happy Birthday, Jesus,' and all the animals got quiet."

"Really, Frankie?" I asked, beginning to believe. "Did the animals sing and talk? Did you understand them?"

"Yes I did. It was wonderful. Didn't you hear them too, Mama?" Frankie asked as he picked up his pillow. "Well, goodnight guys. I'll see you tomorrow." He headed to the house and his warm bed.

I sat on the steps, wondering. Had my son heard the animals speak or had it been a dream? Had God shielded Frankie in his innocence and given him the earnest desire of his heart, which was to sing Happy Birthday to Jesus at midnight with his animal friends?

A mother's heart thinks so.

~ Sharon Blackstock Dobbs

◆ 3 ◆

Come, Adore Him

I'm going for a walk," I told my husband one Christmas morning. "I need to get out of the house and talk with God."

As I trudged along in the brisk mountain air, I bemoaned the fact that we wouldn't see our children and grandchildren that day. I wouldn't get to watch the little ones open presents with glee. I wouldn't get to enjoy pecan pie and candied sweet potatoes with our family. I wouldn't hear "Merry Christmas, Mom," as we walked through the door. I wouldn't be a part of the family interaction with their stories and kidding, as they gathered together. No "Wow, Grandmother, your tree is sure pretty." I wouldn't receive any hugs and kisses from my loved ones. The mailed presents had already arrived at their homes, but I didn't get to see their brightened faces when they opened the gifts. Would they have time to call us between their activities? The fun of Christmas had evaporated for me this year.

God, I believe you want us to live here, but I didn't realize how much I'd miss our children and the family gatherings.

We now lived in Montana, 1,200 miles from our children's homes. Many wonderful people had shared meals and visits in this northwestern area, but it wasn't the same as being with our family. Venturing into Yellowstone National Park and the Big Horn Mountains, whether by vehicle or foot, was great fun. Seeing bear, elk, or big horn sheep was always a thrill. My reminiscing didn't abate my sad feelings. Tears welled up as I talked to God about my misery.

I don't like feeling this way on Christmas day, Lord, please help me.

Suddenly, the strains of "O Come, All Ye Faithful" floated to my ears. A local church broadcasts a hymn at nine o-clock each morning; today, the chimes played that wonderful Christmas hymn. Continuing to walk, I hummed along and my mind recalled the words.

Uh oh. I realized I had allowed the wrong focus to dominate my thinking. Christmas is the remembrance of Jesus' birth — about my caring, loving Savior. My thoughts had centered on my selfish ideas of a perfect Christmas day.

"Oh Lord, I'm so sorry." The reason for my unhappiness was me, not my physical location. The good news was — I could change myself and my attitude. I turned and headed home.

The rest of the day was joyous as I reflected on Jesus' sacrifice for me and I honored him with praise and thanksgiving for coming to earth for me. Then I read from the Bible and continued reading a book about Israel's history, and enjoyed watching a Christmas movie on television. I fixed my husband and myself a simple meal, all the while realizing I was blessed with health, finances, peace, family, and friends.

"Come, adore Him" became my mantra that day and for many following days. I didn't need a big meal and family gift exchange to enjoy Christmas. All the paraphernalia associated with Christmas — the giving of gifts to family and friends, sharing a huge meal with elegant deserts, making fancy cookies, and sending cards of greeting — had overshadowed my thankfulness for Christ coming to earth to redeem me.

Sharing Christmas with others is grand, but it isn't necessary in order to celebrate and worship. Simply...*come and adore Him.*

~ Helen L. Hoover

Happy Birthday, Jesus!

The Christmas after my grandfather died, Mama invited her half-sister to spend Christmas with our family.

I was only six years old at the time, but I remember the confused look on my aunt's face when my Grandmother walked out of the kitchen holding a beautifully decorated birthday cake. When she placed the cake on the table I could read the words, "Happy Birthday, Jesus."

Bending over, I blew the candles out. The family then sang "Happy birthday to you, happy birthday to you, happy birthday, dear Jesus, happy birthday to you."

My aunt scratched her head in confusion. "Why do you do this?"

"To remember that Jesus is the reason we celebrate Christmas. We don't want to leave him out of his own birthday celebration."

Daddy picked up his Bible, turned to the Christmas story in Luke, and began to read about the birth of Christ.

Fast-forward more than 30 years and this is a custom we still practice today with the next generation. After dinner we light the candles on the birthday cake, or birthday cookie, and gather around to sing, "Happy Birthday." The children assemble around the kitchen table and blow out the candles. Then, just as when I was a child, we listen to the reading of the Christmas story.

Jesus humbled himself to become a man before sacrificing himself on the cross for our sins. He suffered and died for our sins, so the least I can do is take a few moments to honor him on the day set aside to celebrate his birth.

~ Diana Leagh Matthews

A Dog, a Broken Boy and a Beer Truck

S now was piled everywhere that Christmas Eve night as we trekked across the almost empty parking lot of the hospital where our daughter, Heidi, was part of pediatrics head-trauma team.

"Snow is magical!" our normally skeptical preteen son announced.

His younger sister agreed. "Can't wait for tomorrow so we can go sledding!"

We each carried some of the hot meal we were bringing to our daughter so we could share at least part of Christmas Eve with her.

As we approached the Emergency Room entrance (the only entrance unlocked at 11:00 p.m.), we stopped in our tracks. A huge delivery truck with a beautiful picture of a team of massive Clydesdale horses, complete with white fetters, idled with parking lights on, next to the ER sliding doors.

"Can't say I've ever seen a beer truck delivering here," my husband quipped.

The glass doors opened and we kicked snow from our boots before going in. The ER was quiet, and the nurses waved and wished us Merry Christmas as we passed by. My husband, Ken, and I served as hospital chaplains and had worked with most of the staff at some point.

Tonight we also wanted to call on six-year-old Timmy, who had been wrapped in bandages in the Pediatric Intensive Care Unit since October, and remained locked in terror of his savage injuries.

Earlier in day, Heidi had called and asked for special prayers because Timmy's fever was spiking. They were having trouble getting it under control.

"Is Timmy responding at all?" I asked.

"No. He stays turned toward the wall, and says not a word. Once this morning, though, he did nod when I asked something. But that is all. Oh, Mom, it's so sad." I could hear the tears of compassion in her heart.

She often called for prayer for the little ones she loved so much. Many of the children had serious, life-threatening situations that required long stays.

19

We had been praying with her for Timmy for some time now.

Timmy and his sister, Leah, had been playing outside their South Dakota farm home one day in October when two stray dogs came into the yard. Their mom, Sarah, was working at the sink by the kitchen window and saw the stray dogs moving into the yard.

She wondered why their two big German Shepherd watchdogs had not chased them away. Generally, if any strange animal came into the yard, both of their dogs would not hesitate to chase after them with great gusto until the offenders were outside the fence line of their property. But that morning, both watch dogs stood near the house, growling at the invading dogs but not moving toward them. Sarah didn't like the looks of that scene.

Leah and Timmy, busy building a snowman, weren't particularly frightened by a couple of stray dogs. As Sarah watched in horror, however, one of the dogs turned toward Leah and pushed her down onto the snowy ground. The other dog ran at her and tried to bite her tiny face.

This spurred the watchdogs into action. They charged the two dogs attacking Leah, which caused one of the dogs to turn toward Timmy, knock him down and bite at his face, while the other stray fought the other watchdog.

Sarah sprang into action, hoping she could get the big dog away from Timmy's face. Timmy's heavy snowsuit protected his neck, but the dog quickly pulled off his hood, baring his head and face. Timmy began screaming as Leah ran toward the house.

Sarah raised sheep and goats and often had to protect their vulnerable animals against predators. An unloaded rifle hung by the back door. It seemed to take forever to pull down the big gun and load the chamber.

Beads of perspiration spilled out across Sarah's forehead as she heard Timmy's continuing cries of fear and pain. she went out onto the porch and called to Leah. "Run, Leah, Run!"

As soon as Leah was clear, Sarah took careful aim with the rifle. The dog was squarely straddling Timmy. There was no room for error. She took a breath, asked for God's grace, and carefully aimed. As she pulled the trigger, she prayed that the bullet would hit the dog's mid-back and not Timmy. The force of the bullet literally blew the dog off Timmy and onto the ground beside him. That allowed Sarah to get off her second shot through its neck. At the sound of the shots, the other dog took off running with the watchdogs in pursuit.

Sarah grabbed her mobile phone and dialed 911 as she ran to Timmy. He lay still, his heavy snowsuit covered with blood. Sarah couldn't tell how much of the blood was his, and how much came from the dog.

She made sure the dog was dead, then threw down the gun. Timmy's breaths were spasmodic. Gurgling sounds were coming from his throat. "Be right back, Timmy. I'm going to go get some blankets to wrap around you 'til the Care Flight comes. Love you."

She ran past Leah, who stood on the porch paralyzed with fear as she stared at her motionless brother on the ground. "Timmy's alive," Sarah told her. "Watch for the helicopter. It's on the way."

Sarah returned with the blankets. Timmy's face and head were torn badly. Blood gushed from multiple injury sites. Sarah pressed towels into the most gaping wounds and whispered constantly to Timmy to keep him focused on her loving voice. "The doctor is on the way, Timmy. He will help you. Mommy is right here."

That day Heidi, as head trauma specialist, was on the helicopter as it sped toward Sarah's farm. "It took 22 long minutes to arrive at the farm. When we first arrived, I didn't think Timmy had much of a chance to survive the terrible head injuries and extreme blood loss. I was praying that the extremely cold weather might at least help slow down this boy's bodily processes and bleeding," she later told us.

Sarah and Leah were fit in tightly on either side of Timmy as the copter rose into the air and Heidi hooked Timmy up to oxygen and intravenous pain medication. She prayed aloud for God's help. Sarah rubbed Timmy's cold hands and sobbed quietly as they flew. Heidi called ahead to request Dr. MacLaren, a pediatric surgeon, to meet them at the hospital. MacLaren was a gruff older doctor with little bedside manner, but he had a great deal of skill in microsurgery for head trauma in children.

Upon arrival at the hospital, Timmy was taken immediately into surgery. Heidi called and asked us to pray during the long surgery, and our entire congregational prayer chain found their way to their knees for the young boy.

The dog's carcass was taken to the university and checked for rabies. After many hours in surgery, Timmy was admitted to the PICU — Pediatric Intensive Care Unit — under Heidi's supervision.

When he entered the PICU, Timmy's face had 120 stitches in radiating circles all around his eyes, nose and mouth. Skin had been grafted into many of the wounds. A shunt was placed temporarily to remove accumulating fluids. Hundreds more stitches were needed to close the wounds on his arms and hands. His snowsuit had been tough enough to keep the dog away from his neck and stomach areas.

When we saw him the next day on our hospital rounds as chaplains, Timmy lay in the PICU, bandages wrapped over his head, face, and chest. His arms and hands were covered with thick bandages as well.

As the weeks turned into months, Timmy lay there, not speaking a word. The only part of his little face that was visible — that wasn't totally covered with bandages — were his eyes. And sad little eyes they were. No crinkles of a smile. No expression. Just dull little eyes that always looked wary and snapped shut if anyone tried to look directly into them.

My husband and I visited Timmy regularly. Everyone wished there was more we could do to help his parents reach the injured boy inside all those bandages. When anyone tried to encourage Timmy to talk, he turned his face to the wall, and said nothing. His silence was a concern to everyone at the hospital.

Heidi would turn on the television that hung high over Timmy's crib-like PICU bed. He ignored the programs, but she noticed that he seemed to respond to one particular commercial.

Just before Christmas, Heidi told us, "Guess what Timmy likes the most on the television. It's that silly beer commercial with — of all things — that big floppy-eared phony dog on it. I don't think Timmy would find a dog very funny right now. But he does seem to watch and listen when it's on."

When Heidi had told us she would be on duty in PICU on Christmas Eve, we did what we usually did. After leading worship in our small church, we packed dinner and presents and took them to the hospital pediatrics floor to share with Heidi and the other nurses.

And so it was we found ourselves staring at the beer truck idling at the ER entrance late that Christmas Eve.

We hurried to the elevator. As the elevator doors swung open, a person walked out dressed in a furry dog costume with the beer company logo sewn on his chest. He bowed to us and everyone in the lobby, then headed out through ER to the waiting truck. We were mystified.

When we stepped out of the elevator onto the Pediatrics floor, we saw several nurses gathered outside Timmy's door. There was laughter and as we approached, we heard a little voice we had not heard before. As we entered the room, we saw Timmy's eyes blazing with new life through those bandage holes.

"Did you see the big dog?" Timmy asked excitedly. "He came to see me, and look what he brought!"

Timmy pointed his bandaged hand toward the end of his bed. There, perched on the foot of the bed, was a six-foot replica of the walking, talking, beer commercial dog we had just met in the elevator!

Around midnight, when we left Timmy's room, we met his mom going in. She had been there earlier, but left depressed when Timmy had failed to respond even to the presents the family brought. She was now returning because Heidi had called her to come down for a special surprise.

The surprise started with her hearing Timmy's voice — a sound she had not heard for months and had despaired of ever hearing again.

Tears were streaming down her face. And ours.

Heidi called us aside. "We are really mystified about this dog. Did you guys send it? You and Doc MacLaren and I are the only ones who knew that Timmy liked the dog on the commercial." We assured her we had not ordered the beer truck, though it obviously had been an answer for Timmy.

Tears flooded from her pretty green eyes. "Remember I called you for special prayer this morning? Timmy took a turn for the worse. He had been running a lowgrade fever and it spiked quite high, causing convulsions. I called Doc MacLaren, who complained about being called early on Christmas Eve, his day off. You both know what he is like. He comes off as an unhappy gruff old guy. Today was no exception," Heidi continued. "Doc MacLaren lost patience with Timmy."

I closed my eyes against that. "Oh, Heidi, what did the doctor do?"

"He hollered at Timmy," Heidi said. "Doc MacLaren yelled, 'I know you can speak, young man! Now I need some questions answered so I can help you! Speak up!' "

I could hardly believe what Heidi was saying.

Heidi said Timmy turned to the wall as usual, and ignored the doctor. MacLaren moved away from the bed. Heidi, hoping to help, put her face right down into Timmy's little face and quietly asked the same question the doctor had asked. Though Timmy had never spoken a word since he had been admitted to the hospital, he had occasionally answered a question from Heidi with a nod of his head. This morning was no exception. Timmy nodded his head in answer.

"That irritates me," Doc told Heidi. "He'll respond to you, but not to me!"

Heidi continued, "The television had been running the whole time Doc had been there. 'Turn that thing off,' he roared as he moved back toward the bed. Then a strange thing happened. A beer commercial came on the television twice as loud as the program had been. Timmy turned toward the TV and giggled at the big gruff fake dog in the ad. Doc MacLaren looked at the TV and Timmy, and then said, 'Oh, leave the TV on for now!' and walked out.

"That was all," Heidi said. "There were just me and Doc MacLaren in the room. When the big furry dog came to visit Timmy tonight, Doc MacLaren was nowhere to be seen. I called to tell him about it, and he said he didn't know anything about it and hung up."

Heidi's story ended there.

We spread the food and treats out for Heidi and the nurses, wished her Merry Christmas and headed home. As we went through the doors from ER, the beer truck was gone. Snow fell quietly in the hospital parking lot. The warmth of a new sparkle in a little boy's eyes was warming us all as our boots squished in the newly fallen snow in the parking lot.

Timmy began to get better that Christmas Eve. In a few weeks, his wounds were significantly better and within a month he was able to go home. He returned several times for surgeries that restored his face, hands and arms to near normal appearance.

No one ever admitted to having ordered or paid for the dog to come on Christmas Eve. No one admitted to paying for the big six-foot stuffed dog. And according to Heidi, Doc MacLaren went on being just about as gruff as before. But, she thought maybe, once in a while, he was a bit gentler after that night.

Psychologists tell you that if you fear something, the best therapy is often to create new positive memories about that scary something. That night, it was a big fake dog…carried on the beautiful messenger feet of God.

The Bible tells us, "How lovely are the feet of those who bring good news, announcing peace." Perhaps that night it took big, furry, floppy feet to carry kindness to a little boy whose world had gone wrong.

That night was the last Christmas we would spend with Heidi. A careless driver killed her on her way to work at the hospital a few months later. But the glow of kindness we shared in that, her last Christmas with us, continues to warm us all and ease the pain of her loss.

Kindness, it is said, is the oil in the engine of life that makes life worth the living. In one little boy's life, kindness released a powerful element of God's grace and healing that nothing else could have done. Kindness, you see, comes straight from God. It is God's way to deliver grace.

Sometimes God's messengers look like angels.

But one night a while back, God's messengers looked like a beautiful kindly nurse, a gruff old doctor, a beer truck, and a big furry dog with a beer logo on its chest. In some strange way they brought the Spirit of God, and hope, with them.

Sometimes God uses the most unlikely messengers if they are willing.

~ *Mary E. McQueen*

Blue Light Special

It was going to be the best Christmas ever! I just knew it. All 23 of our family members were coming home, including 12 wonderful grandchildren ranging in age from three-months to 25 years.

We made our traditional trek to the Christmas tree farm and picked out the biggest and most expensive tree we had ever chosen.

Nostalgia pervaded the room as we viewed cherished decorations and sparkly lights entwined among the fragrant boughs. We enjoyed our tree while waiting in anticipation for loved ones to arrive. Everything seemed perfect.

Unfortunately, one evening just days before Christmas when we turned the lights on, only the bottom portion lit up. The whole top half of our nine-foot tree was dark.

This could not be!

It was cold and rainy, but my husband donned coat and toboggan and went out into the dark night to buy lights.

When he returned, I breathed a sigh of relief and watched as he painstakingly wound the new lights through the branches, trying not to disturb the ornaments. The clock's hands pointed to midnight when it was finally done. The moment had come to turn on our newly repaired tree. We hit the switch, but to my horror the new lights, the only ones left in the store, were the new "cool white" which looked blue beside the golden glowing ones below.

I know blue-light specials are supposed to signal a good deal, but this wasn't it. "Oh no," I groaned. "It looks horrible." But it was either no lights at all or this weird two-toned tree.

I went to bed dissatisfied and grumpy.

I woke up just about the same way. Picking up my devotional book, I read how God is present in every moment and concerned about every detail of my life. The reading was also about the narrow perceptions we humans tend to have where problems and details are concerned.

Would it have made a difference if I had asked for his perception of the

Christmas tree dilemma? He was there in that moment when the blue lights came on. And so I asked.

The answer came immediately. "*I like it just fine.*"

Well then, I mused. *If God likes the tree, who am I to complain?*

I left the bedroom and went out to turn on and enjoy our two-toned tree — our blue light special — the best ever!

~ Charlotte Burkholder

Christmas and Santa

Santa was always a big deal at my house. Not because we didn't celebrate the true meaning of Christmas, though. We read the story of Christmas in the Gospel of Luke. We sang hymns, went to see Christmas lights and participated in church services.

However, we also looked forward to Santa's visit.

Shopping for those special things to go in stockings was something my mom had taught me well. I bought lots of little things I knew my son would like, such as miniature toys of his favorite batman, pizza flavored Pringles, and a small can of regular Coke, which was a rare treat at our house.

We probably overdid it sometimes, but we loved seeing the excitement on our son's face Christmas morning. Santa once assembled an entire Little Tikes playground square in out living room. Another Christmas Santa stayed up most of the night putting together the talking rescue heroes tower. One of my favorites was when Santa put up a two-man tent in the living room complete with sleeping bag, pillow, toy lantern and binoculars.

We spent half the morning playing in the tent. My son was in kindergarten and I remember him saying, "I know Santa is real now cause he put up a tent!" He thought that tent was the best gift, and impossible for anyone to install other than Santa.

A few years later, when he was in third grade, he learned that his parents were, in fact, bringing Santa surprises. I told him that Santa represented the spirit of giving and making our loved ones happy. I also told him that God knows us better than anyone and blesses us with good things. I explained to him that he could be a Santa-giver and fill Christmas stocking with surprises for his dad and me.

He is now 22 years old and we still enjoy stocking stuffer shopping. He always gets my favorites, which are chocolate covered marshmallow candy and dark chocolate. I get every variety of Reece's. Occasionally my son may still find those pizza flavored Pringles and a glass bottle of coke in his stocking.

It's a special time when we consider the other person and the things they love.

Christ came and was a gift to us because of God's love for us. The gift of the Christ child and angels singing was a glorious surprise to the shepherds. The Star of Bethlehem was likely a surprise to all who saw it. Giving gifts to express affection for loved ones seems like good reminders of God's love for us. The wise men brought expensive gifts that were of personal meaning to the Christ Child, our Savior.

As long as I am able, I will continue being a giving-Santa and share God's love and grace with my friends and family.

~ Dorothy Floyd

Christmas in the Ghetto

One of the most sacred and memorable holidays is Christmas. Christians annually pay special homage to the birth of our Savior and Lord on Christmas day by reading about the birth of baby Jesus, singing Christmas carols, and attending Christmas Eve worship services.

I have enjoyed numerous traditions that have developed over the years in the broader celebration of Christmas, like choosing a Christmas tree and then decorating it with lights, ornaments and whatever else we choose.

Then there are the presents.

Although the debate about the commercialization of Christmas continues, giving and receiving presents is a meaningful way to express our love to our family and friends.

Santa and his elves have worked around the clock checking their lists to see who was naughty or nice, while Rudolph and his comrades have been put through rigorous training preparing for a 24/7 week of selecting, wrapping, loading and delivering their special order to children around the world.

There are yummy culinary delights consumed only at this time of the year: delicious treats like eggnog, those rare seasonal flavors of ice cream like spumoni and winter white chocolate, fruit cake, candy canes, and red velvet cake — yummy! Each of us could easily expand this list as we describe our personal and memorable family traditions.

The composer of the words, "I'll be home for Christmas, if only in my dreams," expresses that Christmas is indeed a special time of year like no other.

I recall one Christmas that was far different than what I had grown accustomed to while living in the Carolinas. I was attending Gordon-Conwell Theological Seminary located north of Boston. My academic advisor, professor, mentor and friend was one of the most unique and spiritually challenging men I ever met. His name was Dean Borgman. I could write a whole book on the impact he has had on lives all over the world, especially on the lives of those who lived in the hood. Through the years, Dean has ministered in numerous ghettos across

America, in particular Boston's South End and New York's Harlem.

Dean challenged me to take a course on Urban Ministry. I soon learned that this course was much more than reading several textbooks supplemented by hearing lectures by several authorities describing what it was like to live in the inner city. He exposed his students to everything one might imagine that occurred in the ghetto.

Our highlight was what he described as an Urban Plunge. Basically he was asking us to experience homelessness first hand. The initial requirement was to find food and shelter to sustain our survival. We quickly learned he was serious about his version of urban survival as we surrendered our wallets, watches, car keys and any form of currency we had from cash to credit cards.

He then gave each of us our living wage for this ordeal — a whopping 50¢. Someone inquired if that was for a cup of coffee or a phone call every couple hours. He responded, "No, that is your total living wage until your Urban Plunge is over.

Dean Borgman made us dress for the part. Our tattered winter wardrobe consisted only of what we could wear or carry, no suitcases permitted.

The day came when we were assigned where we would temporarily reside. We soon discovered our class would be scattered all over Boston. Boston is a very diverse city with neighborhoods settled ethnically, politically, economically and in countless other ways.

My new stomping ground became what was known as The Combat Zone. It was appropriately named and no further explanation was needed.

I was always freezing cold despite wearing seven layers of clothes. My two meals per day usually consisted of watered down soup, two sandwiches made from stale bread and a cup of coffee. It seemed that I was constantly in need of the restroom which is a huge challenge when there are few-and-far-between restrooms available for the homeless, especially in the winter.

I also learned that when you are in the hood you are wise not to look into someone's eyes. I eventually avoided all eye contact with others whether they were gang members, police, vagrants or businessmen and families.

Several people, labeled as being financially well off, treated me with contempt. To some extent I had expected that to occur. Now I wondered if, having come from an affluent family, I had treated the homeless the same way through the years.

What I did not expect was what occurred when I ventured into a church to pray. I must admit I relished those few moments of warmth while in there. I found a peace by sitting among the sounds of silence in an empty church. Daily, I was learning valuable lessons about surviving in the ghetto that is never taught in textbooks, or imagined.

Those individuals who reside in the ghetto do not celebrate Christmas in the same manner that most of us have become accustomed to. There is no Christmas Eve service, no cookies and milk for Santa, no decorating a Christmas tree, no warm meal with enough leftovers to feed an entire football team. The most evident difference was that there was no exchanging of presents — none.

I sat in a large room with 60-plus homeless men (some literally wearing rags for shoes) watching *The Price Is Right*. No one talked during the entire show. I looked at the beautiful models smiling and displaying prizes. The first showcase included a brand new car, a new living room, a trip to Jamaica and a cash prize of $25,000. That roomful of men would be wondering where they would they get a meal and warm, dry place to sleep.

An unusual thing happened during the next commercial. A young man in his mid-thirties gave me a present — a small tube of toothpaste and a toothbrush wrapped in cellophane.

I had walked down a darkened alley with this new-found friend. He had learned how to stay alive in the ghetto and was continually advising me what to do and not do. One evening as we were walking through the ghetto, a large, muscular man was brutally punching a young girl. I started to walk across the alley to come to her rescue but my friend said, "Relax, man. He won't kill her because she is his source of income; but if you interfere he won't hesitate to kill you."

Later that evening I sat in a roomful packed to capacity. No one spoke, not even in a whisper. Eventually a large black man who reminded me of the song, "Bad, Bad, Leroy Brown" stood and broke the silence! He softly said, "Men, I want your attention." Every eye turned as if he was an Army Master

Sergeant. He then introduced a young prostitute to the group saying she had never received either a birthday or Christmas present in her life.

He asked for a knife to cut a cake he had gotten somewhere (perhaps stolen) but no one responded. He became upset. In a tone similar to that of a roaring lion he again said, "Someone, give me a blankety-blank knife. Now!"

Thirteen switch blades immediately clicked opened.

He then told all of us to sing Happy Birthday and wish her a Merry Christmas. As we sang, she cried. Tears rolled down my cheeks as well. It seemed as if every man in the room was misty-eyed.

He then turned to us, saying, "Thanks guys, Merry Christmas to all of you."

Something strange happened shortly after. The silence which was prevalent morning, noon and night was broken. A few men began to talk to each other, then more and more began to converse. I looked around and saw several men smiling. I had never seen anyone smile during my time in the ghetto. A few men hugged one another.

Throughout the room people were shaking hands and saying, "Merry Christmas." Conversations continued long into the evening. There was even laughter. Laughter! Can you imagine laughter in a room full of broken and socially discarded men who had learned never to trust anyone! I was in awe as a small group gathered in the corner and sang Christmas carols.

The man who had given me a toothbrush extended his hand and wished me a Merry Christmas. He then whispered, "I don't know who you are. I don't know what you're up to and why you're here but one thing for sure. You're not here by mistake. You're here for a reason."

As I lay in the shelter's bunk that night, reflecting on all that occurred, my thoughts continually returned to what was shared by my friend, "You're not here by mistake. You're here for a reason."

It was as if God had whispered into my ear at that very moment, saying, "Tommy Scott Gilmore, you are here for a reason and it's not to impress Dr. Borgman, or write a paper about the homeless, or even to have empathy for those living like this. Your reason is to tell others about the birth, life, death, and resurrection of Jesus. They need to know the reason for this season."

~ Tommy Scott Gilmore, III

Dashing Through the Snow

Our family had enjoyed giving Christmas gifts secretly to those less fortunate in previous years, so we looked forward to doing it again this year. Each time we chose individuals or a family who probably would be receiving little or nothing for Christmas.

Because we live in a town with a population of 400, news gets around. It wasn't hard finding someone to whom we could take gifts. This year, we chose a young single mother with three children.

We had fun choosing presents for all the family members. We couldn't give expensive gifts, but we looked for things each would enjoy. We packed the presents into a box, along with homemade cookies and candy.

Waiting until after dark on Christmas Eve, we walked through the snow and piled into our car, giggling about what we were about to do. Slowly we drove past the house, waiting for the perfect moment to sneak the gifts to their back porch, knock on the door, and quickly drive away.

However, our plan didn't go as smoothly as we'd hoped. The mother must have seen us driving by, then my young son sneaking to their porch…and became afraid. She phoned her father, who arrived quickly in his pick-up.

We knew he had a reputation for losing his temper, and he had a gun, so it was our cue to make a fast getaway.

He sped after us.

We tried to lose him by driving through the countryside. We drove much faster than we should have, but he stayed right behind us.

Realizing the man was overweight and fearing he might have a heart attack, we decided to head for home so he would give up the chase. But as I pulled into our driveway, he followed closely behind.

He was very angry. He demanded to know what we had been doing at his daughter's house. So we had to confess what we had done.

Much to our relief, after hearing our explanation, he promised he wouldn't tell his daughter that we had left the Christmas box.

No one in our family has forgotten that Christmas long ago when we went dashing through the snow trying to make our unsuccessful getaway.

Scripture encourages us to give gifts in secret. Sometimes it's really hard. Still, it's fun to try giving anonymously.

~ Norma C. Mezoe

The Night Jesus Was Born

Come along with me and I'll be your guide for a walk through one night, 2,000 years ago, a very special night that changed the world forever. As you walk along, consider all the things you see, hear, smell, and touch.

First, what do you see?

Walk along the trail into Bethlehem and look out over the beautiful fertile hills. Here you'll see Bethlehem nestled as a quiet little village.

As darkness begins to swallow up the day, look around quickly. In the surrounding fields, shepherds pasture their flocks. As you walk down the dusty streets to enter the little town, you will notice people rushing to find a place to stay. They've been summoned here to register for taxation.

Glance up. The glorious heavens stretch out like a drape of black velvet, poked with holes for the stars to sparkle through like bazillions of twinkling lights, choreographed as a dance of angels with flashlights.

One divinely-appointed star blazes unusually bright; its brilliance illuminates a lowly stable. Follow the star's beam to the stable.

As you near the stable, stop to listen!

What do you hear?

Heavenly songs of praise ascend above the fields, filling the night's atmosphere with angelic voices.

Now, slowly approach the stable and stand in the entrance. What sounds emanate from within? The gentle lowing of the cattle. The bleating of the sheep. The braying of the donkeys.

Suddenly, the cries of a newborn resonant above all the other sounds.

Step inside.

Listen to the crunch of the straw beneath your feet. Hear the nighttime creatures scurry away at your coming. Become aware of the owl hooting his warning of your presence.

Now stop!

What do you smell?

It's a stable. You know there are odors here! You breathe in the smell of, well, you know. Okay. What other fragrance is there? The aroma of freshly tossed hay.

Step further still into the stable.

There's one gentle, sweet smell...that of a newborn baby. The animals gather around to sniff at this strange little wonder now occupying their trough.

A young woman named Mary has just given birth to the Savior of the world. Swaddling him lovingly, she places him in the trough, and there, the miracle of the manger has taken place.

Join the animals. Lean over the manger. Breathe in that precious earthly, yet divine, scent of an infant.

So, what do you touch?

Your knees gently lower and rest upon the hay beside the manger. You reach out to touch the tiny, pink fingers protruding from the depths of the manger. And now...

What do you feel?

As you've walked the path to Bethlehem, seen the sights, listened to the sounds, smelled the aromas, and touched the treasures of this night, did it all take your breath away? What do you now feel?

Is your heart now so full that you think it will explode? Look around to make a memory of all you have experienced. Allow it all to reside in your heart's manger. Don't ever let these images escape your grasp.

May your Christmas be filled with precious memories and a special touch of the Lord's presence.

~ Lynn Mosher

Wings of Peace

Three o'clock Christmas morning and not a creature was stirring, except me. I had been up for hours nervously watching my seven-week-old baby sleep in a carrier next to my bed.

Glancing at the clock again, I mentally calculated the number of hours since Caleb's last feeding. Almost three hours had passed. He would be awake any minute to be nursed again, and I still had not fallen back asleep. I wondered how long this crippling anxiety would last.

I leaned over to check on our infant son once again and woke my husband in the process.

"Is he up already?" my husband asked quietly, rolling over to lie next to me.

"No, I was just checking on him. He should be awake soon though."

I felt my husband's warmth as he put his arm over my side. "Go back to sleep, he's fine." He sounded confident, relaxed. My husband sure wasn't missing any sleep, or checking Caleb's breathing repeatedly.

It was strange, because I had never felt this fear with our first son. I don't recall checking his breathing or staying awake between his feedings. I never once researched topics like SIDS or crib death statistics while my baby napped.

But Caleb was special. It had taken us almost five years to get to this point after years of infertility problems and two miscarriages. When I was finally able to sustain a pregnancy, my doctor detected some issues on my sonogram, and he warned us our son might be born with medical issues. I had refused further testing during my pregnancy due to the risk of possible miscarriage, so I spent the last five months wondering, and praying that our baby would be all right.

When Caleb was born, he was perfectly healthy, with not a single issue. But I could not get past the fear.

I heard him stirring, making those sounds he would utter right before he let out a full-blown cry of hunger.

My husband gave me a soft kiss on my neck. "Merry Christmas," he muttered. "I'll change him and bring him to you in bed. Just rest."

I had not shared my crippling, and completely unreasonable fear with Bill. I knew he would not understand. He rarely worried about anything.

As I nestled Caleb against me to nurse, I again prayed that God would keep him safe. But even more so, I prayed for reassurance that our son would be protected, and that I would begin to enjoy the baby we had waited for so many years to have.

A few hours later, I awoke to the sounds of my husband and 10-year-old son, Collin.

"Let Mom sleep. She was up several times with the baby." I heard my husband whisper none too softly.

"It's alright. I'm awake." I uttered as I dragged myself out of bed. Ten years old or not, I was sure my oldest son was waiting to open presents. It was Christmas morning after all.

Caleb was particularly cheerful that morning, as if knowing it was a special day. I watched him smile at me after I finished his morning feeding and headed to our dining room where the Christmas tree and gifts were waiting. Collin was already in place on the floor next to the stocking and gifts that bore his name.

"Here, hold your brother next to his stocking so I can take your pictures." I passed the baby to Collin, and watched as he gave his little brother a gentle kiss on the top of his smooth head.

I took a few pictures, and we placed Caleb in an infant bouncy seat in front of the tree. He wasn't exactly going to open gifts, after all. My husband started to pass out the presents, most of which went to Collin.

Sitting quietly on the couch, I watched Collin open his gifts. His excitement was contagious, despite my exhaustion. "Look Mom, I got the Lego Eiffel Tower!" He practically shouted. "And the *Guinness Book of World Records*!"

Soon, all the gifts had been opened, and all that was left was a giant pile of torn wrapping paper in our front hallway. I watched our cat, Sarah, dive in the mess for a strand of curly ribbon. My husband walked past me behind the Christmas tree to gather a few stray pieces of paper. And the rest happened so quickly, I wasn't even sure what I had just seen.

In all the commotion of the morning, I had forgotten that I had purchased my husband a cast iron pie iron. We had just put in an outdoor fireplace, and

I figured he might get a kick out of baking some pies outside on an open fire. I watched as my husband lifted up the heavy, awkwardly wrapped package.

"What's this?" He asked as I saw the heavy iron fall out of its package, right onto my infant son's head, before sliding off the infant seat to the floor.

"Oh God!" came my immediate pleading prayer. "Caleb!" I shouted, fell to my knees on the floor to pick up our crying son. All three of us reacted quickly, gently placing Caleb on the floor to examine him for injury. I pulled back as my husband carefully inspected his head, truly expecting blood or something much worse. I could not stop shaking, imagining horrific damage to my baby's gentle skull.

"There isn't a mark on him." My husband said far more calmly than we all appeared. Caleb's crying had already stopped.

"What do you mean? That heavy thing just fell right on his head! I saw it!" I refused to believe my infant son had escaped this accident unscathed. "Check the back of his head." I demanded.

My husband picked up our baby and handed him to me. "See for yourself, he's fine."

I started checking him myself. I gently felt his entire head for bumps. Caleb just grinned at me.

I looked up at my husband, who was still standing next to Caleb's infant seat, right next to our Christmas tree. I saw the *Baby's First Christmas* ornament I had carefully placed front and center on our tree. Right next to that ornament was a small glass angel, illuminated with yellow light from a nearby strand of lights. As I stared at that little angel, I saw the glass wings move several times against the branches of the tree.

"Did you see that?" I whispered.

"What?" my husband asked.

"Nothing."

I felt a wave of peace the likes of which I had never experienced before. I just knew: Caleb was protected. There was no way he could have escaped injury without heavenly protection.

That night, I slept without fear for the first time in months. I never spent another night checking on my son. I knew he was safe.

~ Denise Valuk

The Glitter Light

I was happy to be spending Christmas with my family. My husband, two children, and I were at a local nursing home delivering our cards, which we make out of recycled cards from Christmases past. We look forward to this tradition every year and feel blessed to visit our elderly friends.

It was always rewarding to see the look on the residents' faces when they realized we made special Christmas cards just for them to enjoy. Many times they gave hugs and kisses in appreciation. Seeing such a small act of kindness so greatly appreciated by those in the facility was heart-warming.

As much as I love this family tradition, it can be a little depressing at times. The nursing home we usually visit is in desperate need of repairs. The paint has faded, the decorations are sparse, and it lacks that warm, cozy feeling of home. Some of the rooms don't have many personal items like family photos or pretty figurines and plants. The rooms seem bare and lonely, just as some of the elderly do.

However, on this particular visit to the home, we came upon a room at the very end of the hallway with the door cracked just a bit. This room appeared to be like all the others, nothing special about it. There was no decoration on the outside of the door. It had the familiar wood grained finish and room number plaque beside it.

I knocked and heard a feeble voice say, "Come on in." I opened the door and introduced myself to the woman in bed, and then proceeded to explain the reason for our visit. I was giving the red, handmade card to the woman when something bright and spectacular caught my eye. In the corner of this woman's humble room sat the most beautiful angel lamp I've ever seen.

The top of the angel was adorned with white sparkles and she wore a shiny, golden halo. Her skirt appeared to have a million brilliant specks of glitter swirling around in dazzling fluid. The combination of the light and sparkle were breathtaking and wonderful, giving off a brilliant cascade of perfectly speckled light on the ceiling and walls.

I didn't want to stop looking at the lamp. It was stunning.

But as I continued to stare at the angel, I thought that beautiful angel shouldn't be in this indifferent, gloomy room. The space was ugly and undeserving of the precious light from this wonderful piece. I suddenly caught myself wishing I could rescue the angel, that I could take her somewhere else, anywhere else would be better than here.

Then I was ashamed for having those thoughts. I'm sure that the angel lamp brought much happiness to the woman. I'm certain the light the angel provided somehow warmed the lady's soul and maybe brought her back to memories of happier times in her life. I don't know the story behind how the woman came to acquire this lamp but I am sure it had significant meaning to her.

Since that day, I have thought about the lamp many times. I named the lamp The Glitter Light when describing it to others. It is still the prettiest angel figurine I have ever seen. As the lamp continues to be vivid in my memory, the Lord has reminded me of important things during the Christmas season.

The reason for this holiday is to celebrate the birth of Jesus Christ. God sent his perfect, amazing, beautiful son to our world... our cold, dark, ugly world. Jesus didn't belong on earth, for he was too perfect, too Holy to be here. But God sent him anyway, because it was part of his plan for our salvation. The Bible tells us in John 8:12 (NLT), Jesus said to the people, "I am the light of the world. If you follow me you won't be stumbling through the darkness because you will have the light that leads to life." Jesus came to earth to be our light so we would never have to face the darkness of our sins.

How thankful I am that God made the sacrifice of sending his blessed son to my dark, sinful world so I may have the eternal life his light offers. Just as the angel lamp seemed out of place in that nursing home room, Jesus' light seemed out of place on earth when he was born. I'm so thankful that God didn't rescue his son, as I wanted to rescue the angel from that bland room.

If God had rescued Jesus, we never would be able to experience his full light, the light that is even more brilliant and breathtaking than the angel lamp could ever be.

~ Alisha Ritchie

Christmas with Grandkids

Ho-Ho-Ho shouts the voice from the TV,
I turn my head to listen for he is surely talking to me.

With the flip of the calendar the jolly season draws near,
no matter what the weather, it's time for a cup of good cheer.

We've made our lists and we're checking them twice,
while we caution the grandkids to not be naughty but nice.

With the dawning of December we've hit more than one store,
hoping to find Christmas bargains galore.

But everywhere we went not a parking space could be found,
so we followed fellow shoppers as they circled round and round.

Being a grandparent makes Christmas all the more merry and bright.
Our munchkins and their smiling faces always make for a happy sight.

Shopping for the kiddies is oh so much fun,
and I'm just getting started so I am far from done.

Their eyes light up with wonder when speaking of the Elf on the Shelf.
I can't help but get caught up in the giddiness in spite of myself.

This year little hands helped decorate our house for the season,
with Christmas characters placed here, there and everywhere
with no rhyme or reason.

It didn't matter that their "help" created more of a mess.
To me the house never looked more beautiful, I must confess.

When you're a grandparent you see Christmas through fresh eyes,
and the kid in you is born again — oh what a welcomed surprise!

The house is now all cozy and festive in all it's Christmas splendor,
thanks to wee little ones, so loving and so tender.

Grandkids are the gifts that keep giving from one year to the next,
though as I glance at photos from past holidays I sometimes feel perplexed.

Someday I know there'll come a Christmas when my presence won't be seen,
that's when I hope the memories will bring happiness for them to glean.

But that's not what I dwell on when snowflakes start to fall,
for being a grandma at Christmas is the greatest gift of all.

Christmas is a present that stays forever wrapped up in your heart,
and each time that we reopen it we unwrap a whole new start.

Each time I flip the calendar to the month of December,
I smile because I know it will be a Christmas to remember.

Tis the season to be jolly to shop and wrap and bake,
To hang stockings, sip hot chocolate and sing carols for goodness sake.

There's nothing more meaningful than being a grandparent

~

And especially at Christmas it rekindles a soft and lasting glow,
for the love you have for your children's children will never cease to flow.

May the beauty of Christmas surround you with happiness and love,
as we stop to thank the One who gives all blessings from above.

~ Kathy Whirity

14

Reliving a 1947 Small Town Christmas Season

Christmas Day in 1947, when I was five years old, was on a Thursday. Back then, my father was the young pastor of an Assemblies of God church in Truesdale, Iowa. This tiny hamlet of approximately 125 souls was tucked away in the all-encompassing embrace of adjoining cornfields seven miles from Storm Lake in the northwest corner of the state. Even road maps barely bothered to notice it. This sleepy little town's main street consisted of one block of stores and businesses.

Yet, Truesdale's size and isolation didn't keep its inhabitants from coming together during this special season to celebrate the birth of Jesus. Most of our congregation lived out of town alongside a maze of backwoods dirt roads and worked the land for a living.

Though this church was so small it resembled a Holiday Inn room that had been through a compactor, each Sunday it was filled with 70 to 80 people, and often more, which equated to over half the town's population. Our congregation conducted its annual Christmas program on the Sunday evening prior to that Thursday Christmas.

I discovered one picture of that Christmas service in a photo album my mother had kept until she passed away at age 95. It shows a 14-member orchestra playing a song, with my dad seated on the platform behind them, and all of the hard wooden pews filled to capacity. Colorful Christmas bunting is woven tightly around the platform railing. It's also attached in four flowing waves across the entire sanctuary to a lone lamp dangling from the center of the ceiling.

This orchestra presented a special musical program before our congregation was led in singing a selection of Christmas songs. All these years later, I can still recall the joy and enthusiasm with which "Silent Night," "O Holy Night,"

"Away in a Manger," and "O Little Town of Bethlehem" were sung with gusto by these common country folk that wintry evening.

After a short Christmas message from dad, the children's program began, which my mother had directed. My part that year consisted of a couple of sentences I've long forgotten. After everyone had finished their parts, our church superintendent had ushers pass out boxes of candy to each person. This was one of the highlights of my evening. When the service ended, we wished each other a blessed Christmas and went our separate ways. The parsonage was next door so I didn't have to go far.

That year, the Methodist church — the only other church in town — held its Christmas program on Christmas Eve, so my mother took my brother and me to that service, which was my opportunity to receive an additional ration of goodies. There wasn't a lot to do in such a small town so this intermingling of church congregations was a common occurrence.

After walking home through our snow-draped neighborhood, it was time to open presents. Our family never waited until Christmas morning. The usual routine was to gather in our living room while my brother, who was four years older, and I passed out the gifts. Then we would all kneel by the couch while one of our parents offered a prayer.

This particular year, dad had purchased a wind-up 8mm movie camera. While Mom prayed, Dad stood behind us and I could hear the "whirring" of his camera capturing the scene. That's when my juvenile curiosity overwhelmed me and I glanced over my shoulder to investigate this new technology. My lack of reverence and discipline captured on film will forever convict me. This Christmas scene has been shown over and over, through the intervening years, during subsequent family gatherings, and my indiscretion always repeats itself. I still have dad's 8mm projector, too, that he kept until his death at age 91.

My parents took turns filming as each of us opened our gifts that evening. My main present was an electric Lionel train set that included an engine, three cars, and a caboose. It ran on a small round track that snapped together.

For a prolonged period of time, my dad and brother took turns running and playing with this train — until my protests finally brought results and I was allowed to take official ownership. That Christmas season was a special time, on many levels, and my memory often takes me back to these unforgettable moments. It's different today, since I'm the only one left in our family who can appreciate that church service photo, the 8mm film, and our evening of opening gifts. My brother passed away at age 60, after having been a missionary to Nicaragua and Costa Rica for 20 years.

I often think about those stalwart parents in that country church who raised their children in a biblically-based Christian atmosphere. Most of them were surrounded by endless acres of farmland, chickens, pigs, cattle, and the "sshwutt-sshwutt" of cows' milk sloshing into a metal pail. Being surrounded by such people, during that unforgettable Christmas has created a legacy of gratefulness that reaches beyond time and continues to enrich those of us from that original congregation who still remain.

Since then, I've lived around the world on three continents for over 27 years as a military officer and aviator. A few years ago, my wife and I drove from our home in Nebraska to Truesdale for a visit. The former parsonage had been torn down long ago. But that other white structure, displaying its significant cross, still stands on a corner next to the main road. Life in this hamlet has endured drastic changes since I was five. This former vibrant church is now used as a storage center. Life does carry on, with or without us, and things never stay the same.

Today I'm 70 years old and retired from the military. With every Christmas that arrives, I'm flooded by nostalgic memories of those days long past and that unique year when so many wonderful people celebrated the Christmas season together in a country church in small town America.

In my mind I frequently replay our opening of gifts 68 years ago. I've forgiven everyone in my family who played with my Lionel train before I had my turn. And the film to prove that this actually happened, captured with dad's 8mm movie camera, still exists. The truth is that I'd give just about anything to experience those moments with them again. And I wouldn't complain, this time around, about the great train hijacking that occurred in Truesdale, Iowa on that special Christmas Eve of 1947.

Christmas is a bridge.
We need bridges as the river of time flows past.
Today's Christmas should mean creating happy hours for tomorrow
and reliving those of yesterday. -Gladys Tabor

~ Robert B. Robeson

15

The Jesus Jar

The knowledge of Sasha's early passion for jigsaw puzzles should have prepared me for the surprise. But, then who could predict the workings of a six-year-old brain?

With car keys in hand, my son said, "Will you take me shopping? I want to get Jesus a puzzle for his birthday."

Even though our family celebrated Christmas as Jesus' birthday, complete with a cake and candles, Sasha's logical request stunned me into momentary silence. Then our debate began.

"Honey, Jesus lives in heaven which is very far away."

"But, you send presents to Colorado. That's far away isn't it? Why can't we send a puzzle to Jesus?"

Sasha was sure Hank, our mail carrier, knew how to deliver a gift to heaven's door. When he was told there were no roads for Hank to drive on, Sasha's next thought was to talk to Hank's boss. The merry chase of this argument required a quick prayer for wisdom. Unlike a mother-in-training, the Lord was not astonished at the current conversation and already had help on the way.

Music from the radio ceased playing and the familiar voice of a local evangelist filled the kitchen. "Oh listen," I said, "Mr. West is telling people about Jesus again. Did you know he pays money to do this program every week?"

Sasha's eyes narrowed with suspicion, or was it frustration? "Mr. West does this program because he knows it makes God happy," I continued. "I think giving money to Mr. West so he can keep telling people about Jesus would be a better gift than a puzzle. I'm sure this gift would make Jesus smile. And we wouldn't have to mail it to heaven."

With hands on hips to emphasis the gravity of the subject, Sasha asked, "You really think he'd like that better than a puzzle?"

"I do. I really, really do."

Before he could launch a new line of reasoning, I sprang into action. "Let's find a jar, paper, colored pencils and glue."

In bold letters I wrote JESUS on a slip of paper. Sasha drew a Christmas tree with gifts underneath and then glued his label to our jar. Together we came up with jobs like: set the table, make the bed, pick-up my toys. These tasks were listed on construction paper. Each duty completed earned a checkmark worth a quarter. At the end of each week, quarters were counted out and then placed in the jar.

I called Mr. West to explain about the Jesus jar. We set up an appointment to meet at his house one evening for the jar presentation.

The evening of our appointment, Mr. West thanked Sasha, then asked him into the kitchen for a piece of chocolate cake. Sasha sat at the table amazed to hear the familiar voice of Mr. West coming out of his face rather than our radio. From the doorway, Mrs. West and I listened to them talk about the significance of Jesus' birthday. On the way home Sasha said the jar was a good gift and he was sure Jesus was smiling because he liked it.

Years later Sasha's son, Nathan, called to tell me about his plan to bake cookies and brownies to sell along with lemonade at his mom's garage sale. The goal was to earn money for Jacob who lived down the street. This friend needed a bone marrow transplant, which was terribly expensive. When the sale was over, an excited grandson called to tell me, "Grandma, I got $65 to give Jacob!"

Sixty-five dollars wouldn't make much of a dent in the huge medical expenses facing this family. But no longer a mother-in-training, I was better prepared for the wonder of a six-year-old boy's passion to share a special delivery gift in the name of Jesus. Together Nathan and I agreed this was indeed a good idea. We were sure God was smiling.

I've discovered even if a mother, child or grandmother gets confused, needs wisdom and heaven seems too far away, God owns all the puzzling pieces of life and He sees the big picture of how they all fit together generation after generation.

~ *Susan Engebrecht*

16

Remembering the Reason for the Season

M ama and I were excitedly preparing for family to descend on us over the next three days. The day, Friday, had been crazy with work and last minute shopping. After all, Christmas was only three days away, and the house would be wall to wall with family.

We had celebrated Christmas earlier with my sister and her family. She was expecting their third child, a girl. Inducement had been scheduled for two days after Christmas, which also was the wedding anniversary of my sister and her husband.

I was driving home from a long day at work when Mama called me with the news that she'd just received an unexpected phone call. My sister was in active labor. I rushed home and hurriedly packed an overnight bag.

Mama and I sped down the interstate, praying for safety and a healthy delivery for my sister and the baby. Welcoming a new baby is always a wonderful reminder of the things that are important in life. This baby was even more exciting for our family. She would be the first girl born into the family since her mother had graced us with her arrival 28 years earlier. The decision to name my niece after both of her great-grandmothers, who were still living, was an added bonus.

Mama and I arrived safely and were able to have a brief visit with my sister and her husband while we waited for our newest family member to make an entrance.

We were surprised when, 15 minutes after visiting, we were told my niece had arrived. (She rushed into the world and has not stopped since.)

A short while later we were able to hold and coo over our beautiful baby girl. My heart swelled with love for this precious bundle of joy. Holding her in my arms, I thought about the reason for the Christmas season — the birth of our Lord and Savior Jesus Christ.

Holding such a small, innocent treasure caused me to contemplate how Mary must have felt the first time baby Jesus was laid in her arms. The shepherds and angels visited, the same way families and friends visit today.

We are told in Luke that Mary kept all these things, and pondered them in her heart.

May we never forget the true reason we celebrate the season. The birth of Jesus was the greatest gift we have ever been given. In John's gospel, he tells us that God did not send his Son into the world to condemn the world, but to save the world.

I find joy and peace in pondering the real reason for the season.

~ Diana Leagh Matthews

17

Wishbooks and Promises

When I look into the night sky, a precious, childhood memory brings a smile: Dad, Mom, my two brothers and me in the yard of our old farmhouse near the little logging town of Darrington, Washington, gazing into the heavens ablaze with stars. Alan, Randy, and I closed our eyes tight and chanted.

Star light, star bright,
First star I see tonight,
I wish I may, I wish I might,
Have this wish I wish tonight.

Chicken wishbones also bring back memories. I liked it when Mom held one side. She always wished that I would get my wish!

But of all the gifts of wishing, none compared with finding the Christmas wishbooks in our mailbox.

I pressed my nose to the icy window, blew on the glass and called, "Mom, here comes the mailman!" I crammed a stocking cap over my blond hair, shoved my feet into boots, stuffed my arms into my warm coat, and pulled on mittens.

Seconds later, I flew across the big front porch, down the three steps, and plowed into the fresh snow.

It wasn't easy breaking a trail past the pine and fir trees, but I finally got to the mailbox by the edge of the country road. I held my breath and felt the same thrill that came every time I beat Randy and Alan to the box. Then, a quick pull and — "Oh, boy!" I snatched the bulky bundle of mail, shut the mailbox door, and slowly started toward the front porch.

"Hurry up, won't you? Did they come? Why are you so slow?" The shouts from the porch made me grin. I loved my brothers, but we all liked to tease. Whoever brought in the daily mail made the others wait as long as possible before they could find out what had come.

Today I was so excited I sped up. "Look what I found!" I waved a thick catalog, then a thinner one.

"Sears Roebuck and Montgomery Wards both?" Alan grinned, and little Randy danced up and down.

"Yes." I almost dropped the rest of the mail but made it inside, catalogs held away from the boys' reaching hands.

"Mom, tell Colleen to give me a wishbook," Alan demanded.

"Me too," Randy echoed.

Mom just laughed. "No wishbooks until we get our work done. We have to make tree trimmings for Christmas."

Our family had plenty to eat and wear and a good, warm home furnished with love, but there wasn't money for tree decorations.

I turned the wishbooks over to Mom. "It would be awful not to be ready," I said. "C'mon, Alan and Randy, let's get started."

We gathered around the big oak dining room table. Strips of red and green paper waited for the paste to make paper chains. Cranberries and popcorn lay ready for stringing. Shiny tin-can tops with holes that Dad had drilled in them wore pieces of ribbon so they could hang from the Christmas tree branches. When the lamplight reflected on them, they glistened like silver. And long, corkscrew pieces of cans opened with a key also looked silvery.

Alan sighed. "I wish we could have electric lights on our tree."

"We can't have electric lights when we don't have electricity." My fingers busily pasted and hooked paper chains.

"I like the star candles," Randy announced. He had a blob of white paste on his nose, but his eyes shone as blue as the huge star-shaped candles that always burned at Christmastime. He held up a crooked chain with some small loops and some big ones. I looked at Alan. I knew he wanted to laugh as much as I did, but it would hurt Randy's feelings. Instead, I patted my little brother's hand and told him, "Here are some more strips you can paste."

That evening after supper, we moved to the living room. Wood in the big heater gave warmth. Two kerosene lamps on the table drawn near the stove shone on three curly heads. I had the big wishbook. Alan had the thin one filled with toys and wagons and sleds. Mom had dug out a last year's book for

Randy. He didn't know the difference and happily turned pages. "Why is it a wishbook?" he asked.

Dad swung Randy to his lap. "Because when you read it you say, 'I wish I had a wagon,' or 'I wish I had a sled.'" His blue eyes crinkled around the edges.

"I wish I had an elephant."

Alan and I grinned, but Mom said, "It's just a fun game. You know we don't have money for the things you put on your lists." She motioned to the sheets of paper Alan and I were filling with pencil writing. "There's as much chance of Randy getting an elephant as your getting those wishes, at least most of them."

"We know." Alan and I kept writing. We did know, but pretending was fun.

Dad smiled at us. "One of the most beautiful gifts God has ever given us is the gift of wishing. If we use it right, wonderful things can happen. Think of people like Thomas Edison and Benjamin Franklin. They wished they knew more about things and were willing to work hard to find out. That's how electricity was discovered and telephones were invented."

Alan made a face. "Do we always have to work hard when we wish?"

Dad's eyes twinkled." You won't get far without working, Son." He looked at his watch. "Almost bedtime. Leave your wishbooks for tomorrow night."

When we reluctantly put down the catalogs Mom said, "Want to know something special? There's a more important wishbook than all the catalogs put together."

"Really?" Alan and I sat up straight. Randy's half-closed eyes popped open.

"Yes. Wishing can be fun, but promises are better." Mom reached for the big black family Bible. "This is a *Wishbook and Promises* book."

"What are some of the promises?" Randy wanted to know.

"The best promise is that we can have all the joy and love and happiness there is if we follow God's Son, Jesus," Mom quietly said.

Dad pointed to the words Satisfaction Guaranteed on the cover of the nearest catalog. "The Bible doesn't say this on the cover, but God stands behind every one of his promises. His Word never fails."

Long after Dad blew out the lamps, I snuggled under the heavy, handmade quilts on my bed. I thought about what he and Mom had said. Then I whispered, "Wow, a whole Book filled with God's promises! That really is the best wishbook."

The next moment I fell asleep, while heaps and billows of soft snow, to run and play in the next day, fell outside my icicle-hung window.

~ Colleen L. Reece

Sign of True Love

This will be a sign for you: you will find a baby
wrapped in cloths and lying in a manger.
Luke 2:12 (NAS)

E ach year tucked away on a little 12-house court, neighbors display a
lighted version of The Twelve Days of Christmas on their front lawns.
When our children were small we enjoyed driving through the court, singing
the song at the top of our lungs. Although it was a cherished part of our
holiday tradition, I wondered what this carol had to do with the true meaning
of Christmas.

After some research, I was excited to find each symbol had a Christian-
based meaning. Although there is debate as to the origins of this idea, some
believe several centuries ago in England when Catholics were not allowed to
practice their faith they made up a song with secret signs for all the elements
children needed to remember for catechism.

The "true love" mentioned in the song lyrics was, of course, Jesus and his
great love for us. The partridge in a pear tree would also represent Jesus,
crucified on a tree. Two turtle doves were reminders of the Old and New
Testaments. The three French hens symbolized faith, hope and love. Four
calling birds stood for the four gospels of Matthew, Mark, Luke and John.
Each successive verse edified another facet of the Christian faith.

I am so thankful each year for traditions such as nativity scenes, children's
reenactments of the Christmas story, scripture readings and carols that remind
us of the true love that came to earth that starry Bethlehem night.

> Father, I am so thankful for the freedom to express our
> Christian faith in America. I pray we will boldly exercise our
> privilege this season by sharing the beautiful love story of Jesus
> with others. Amen.

~ *Bonnie Mae Evans*

19

Mom's Red Cookie Tin

"Mom, the cut-outs always go in the red tin."

Kate continued opening cookie tins, commenting and checking on the progress of the Christmas baking. "The chocolate oatmeal bars go in the oblong plastic container. The pineapple drops go in the round container." Her tone was a combination of protest and correction. After years of holiday baking, we had a system. In a hurry, I had put the cookies into the wrong containers.

The red tin was my mother's. I remember several containers filled with Christmas cookies when I was a little girl and like Kate, I kept track of the cookies she baked. Even though my mother had worked full time outside the home, she baked during evenings when she came home from work and Christmas baking was a tradition and a delight. Her hand-written list of "Christmas Cookie Baking" is framed and displayed in my kitchen.

Like my mother, I worked outside the home, and I kept her cookie tradition.

Each year my daughters and I baked about 20 varieties of cookies and each, out of habit, had its specific storage container. We'd visit neighbors to deliver plates of cookies and extend wishes for a Merry Christmas. My mother had done the same and though she died before my girls were born, the example of her generosity, recipes, and storage tins connect us to her.

Inevitably, when we're together, we'll share stories associated with a cookie recipe or a delivery. We remember burning the Toffee Bars and throwing out the entire batch. There was the time a widow gave the girls candy canes when they took cookies to her.

One year, to speed up the process, Susan put butter in the microwave to soften. Unfortunately, eggs had already been added and the mixture became scrambled eggs! It wasn't funny then, but we laugh now. Susan has become an extraordinary cook.

I still make some of my mother's recipes, have added some of my own, and often try one new recipe that sparks my interest. I keep a list dated each year. We write notes as a reminder to double the recipe for a particular favorite.

Last Christmas, my youngest daughter had her 20-month-old son watch us bake cookies while seated in his high chair. With our help, he did his share by using the cookie cutter.

I've mentioned downsizing the baking, but Kate won't hear of it. Stories, baking, and time together have made our cookie tradition a non-negotiable part of the Christmas season. "If you do, which ones will you eliminate? The grandchildren won't appreciate the significance. The tradition will be lost."

Today, my daughters are all married. They participate in cookie exchanges and bake and deliver cookies to friends. That may seem unusual now that frozen cookie dough and store bought cookies prevail. But last week, Heather rang a doorbell with her plate of cookies in hand. She introduced herself to her new neighbor.

"What a surprise!" the neighbor said. "How did a young lady like you decide to do this?"

"Well," Heather answered. "My mother always did and we baked as a family every Christmas. She still has her mother's red cookie tin and…"

Legacy: connecting the past with the present and the future.

~ Marilyn Nutter

20

When Christmas Isn't Perfect

I watch as my daughter feeds her newborn, cradled warm and soft against her. A diaper change, then a new, soft onesie. How gently she dresses her, guiding one floppy arm, then the other through uncooperative sleeves.

"There, she's ready," she says, planting a kiss the top of the fuzzy head. "Will you hold her while I get changed?"

Will I hold her? Would I like to gaze deep into a pink sunset or savor something sweet?

"I'd love to," I say, and she settles the baby onto my lap in one smooth motion.

Lauren, the two-year-old, flits by, strokes the top of her baby sister's head like a treasured lovey, and sings the ABC's: "H-I-J-K-LMNOPEEEEEEE."

Somewhere from the nether regions of the baby's diaper, a discordant sound interrupts the alphabet chorus. Lauren stops in her tracks. Her eyes widen as she recognizes the familiar sound.

"Sissy poo poo."

"Yes, Sissy poo pooed," I acknowledge, as warm wetness forms a perfect circle on my leg.

I hand Lauren a wipe, and she cleans her stuffed Minnie Mouse's felt bottom while I gently wipe the chubby cherub who's staring up at me with a self-satisfied smile. I smile in return, shaking my head.

The Christmas season is upon us. Despite road rage and long checkout lines, people smile more. We remember to say *please* and *thank you* and look for opportunities to give sacrificially. We make time to visit with family and friends, and most gatherings are sweet and special.

But every now and then, someone poo poos.

Inevitably something less than idyllic happens to mar the Hallmark-Channel scene. Someone says something unkind, or selfish, or rude. A family member or friend expects to be served rather than serves, takes instead of givies, or criticizes instead of compliments.

When this happens, and it will, we have a choice — focus on what is wrong, or focus on what is right.

We can compile a list a mile long of what's wrong with the world, our lives, or our holiday celebrations. Or we can make an equally long list of what's right. Even if we have to think a bit.

The apostle Paul wisely tells us in Philippians 4:8 (NLT), "Dear Friends... Fix your thoughts on what is true, and honorable and right. Think about things that are pure and lovely and admirable. Think about things that are excellent and worthy of praise."

Thank you, Lord, that Christmas is more than gifts under the tree. Christmas is Christ with us, the hope of glory.

Thank you that we can feel as David, the poet did, in Psalm 40:2: He lifted me out of the pit of despair, out of the mud and the mire. He set my feet on solid ground and steadied me as I walked along. He has given me a new song to sing....

Thank you for our families. Flawed and frustrating though they may be sometimes, they are ours by your design. You have used them in many ways to demonstrate your faithfulness.

Thank you that your mercies are new every morning. Thank you for providing for us all the days of our lives.

Thank you for your Holy Spirit's presence that comforts and consoles, instructs and inspires, and empowers and emboldens. With him, we are never alone.

Thank you for those you've brought into our lives to walk the faith walk with us: spouses, parents, siblings, and friends. Those who love Jesus and love us give us glimpses of what eternity will be like as part of your great big family.

And thank you for Jesus, who binds up the brokenhearted and heals all their wounds.

Merry Christmas.

– Lori Hatcher

21

A Distant Memory

Earth: a distant memory seen in an instant of repose,
crescent shaped, ethereal, beautiful.

~ Alfred Worden

While growing up, my son, Steve, especially treasured Sunday visits with his grandparents. We all relished Grandma's fried chicken and buttermilk biscuits, but for my 10-year-old son the real attraction was the color television Grandpa had installed in their bedroom. Steve doted on *Walt Disney's Wonderful World of Color.*

In those days, only about a quarter of the homes in the U.S. boasted color sets. The rest of us dragged through our evenings watching *The Smothers Brothers, Mission Impossible* and *Mannix* in dull, drab, dreary black and white.

By 1968, color television technology had improved, and some manufacturers had reduced prices. Magnavox, Philco and Zenith competed in advertising their latest stylish consoles. And all three networks began broadcasting prime time shows in color.

My husband, Bob, and I had been paying off some education loans, but now we had a little extra tucked away in our savings account. Bob had read an article in *Popular Mechanics* that predicted this would be the breakthrough year for color, with one manufacturer offering a smaller model for $200.

We debated whether we could afford the splurge. It hadn't been a happy year, with the assassinations of Martin Luther King and Bobby Kennedy. Thousands of Americans were dying in the Vietnam War. We did agree we needed to do something special for Christmas, something that would cheer us up.

"Let's go for it," Bob decided, shortly after Thanksgiving. "Let's get a color television." We both grinned. This would be a huge gift for our family.

The Saturday morning before Christmas we broke the news to Steve. I'd seen his Christmas wish list earlier. He hoped for some Beatles albums, a renewal of his subscription to *Sky & Telescope,* and some rolls of coins to search through in hopes of completing his Roosevelt dime collection.

He certainly hadn't asked for a color television set. I think that possibility seemed as remote to him as men orbiting the moon seemed to me. But he accompanied us when we shopped for the set. We all preferred one polished oak cabinet that housed a 23-inch screen. Steve liked its shelves for storing *TV Guides,* and I liked the doors to shutter the screen when it wasn't turned on. Bob liked its size that was just right to position in a corner of our small apartment living room.

That year, Christmas fell on a Wednesday. Though Steve enjoyed a two-week holiday vacation, I'd have only Christmas day off. Bob, a police officer, worked swing shift, leaving home each afternoon around 2:00 p.m., and returning shortly after 11:00 p.m. He had Sundays and Mondays off.

Steve and I would wait up for him Christmas Eve. We always selected one gift to unwrap on that night. Then we'd all get to bed by midnight. We'd wake early on Christmas morning to open everything that Santa had left, and then head for the grandparents' house for a noontime turkey feast topped off by Grandma's traditional German apple pie.

With Steve's avid interest in astronomy, he could hardly wait for the historic first manned flight to leave the Earth's orbit. On Christmas Eve the three American astronauts aboard Apollo 8 were scheduled to broadcast live photos from nearly a quarter of a million miles away as they orbited the moon. We'd heard that this might be the largest television audience in history so far.

"And to think we'll see it in living color!" Steve confided. "I'm so happy we have the new set."

Christmas Eve night, Steve switched on the Christmas tree lights, and we settled down to enjoy our new television while we waited for Bob's late return. Since the set had been delivered a couple of days earlier, we'd already delighted in catching seasonal old favorites such as *Mr. Magoo's Christmas Carol* and *White Christmas*, marveling at how much we'd missed in previous years when we'd watched in black and white.

The broadcast began. But because of the drabness of the moon, all the footage came to us in simple black, white and subdued shades of gray. Our celestial companion looked to be a dark and unappetizing place indeed.

"Are you disappointed?" I asked, turning toward Steve. "This would have looked just the same on our old black and white set, I'm afraid."

My son, however, seemed mesmerized. His gleaming eyes were glued to the shimmering screen. He held up a warning hand. "Listen!"

I turned back to the TV. At that moment, astronaut William Anders began to speak. "We are now approaching lunar sunrise and, for all the people back on Earth, the crew of Apollo 8 has a message that we would like to send to you. 'In the beginning God created the heaven and the earth.'"

He continued to read from the opening chapter of Genesis. "And God said 'Let there be light!'" Jim Lovell took over next. We listened, enthralled at how the ancient words resonated against the backdrop of the moon and a rising Earth.

Frank Borman read the final few of verses, and then concluded, "And from the crew of Apollo 8, we close with good night, good luck, Merry Christmas, and God bless all of you, all of you on the good Earth.'"

When Bob came home, Steve and I were watching a recap on the late news. "See anything great in color?" he asked.

I shrugged. "We watched Apollo 8. The images were kind of grainy and in black and white."

Then my astronomy-loving 10-year-old spoke up. "It's the most amazing thing I've ever seen, Dad. What a Christmas gift."

"The color TV?"

"No!" Steve chuckled. "The Earthrise! And it's true. It's really round, just like a marble."

The next day, after finishing a meal with the grandparents, Steve — for the first time — didn't bound off to the bedroom. He hung around the table, content to stay close to family, as we indulged ourselves in another dollop of pie.

"Don't you want to watch TV?" Grandpa asked.

"We have a color TV of our own now," Steve replied, shaking his head.

"See any *Wonderful World of Color* on it yet?"

"I'll have to wait until Sunday for Disney. But last night I saw something better."

"Better than Disney? What's that?"

"The Apollo 8 orbiting the moon. I saw our very own wonderful world, in black and white. I saw the Earth rise."

I still can smell our old pine-scented little living room. I still can hear those faraway astronauts' crackling voices. And I still can see that little polished oak cabinet, the twinkling tree, and my son's wonderstruck expression, all in radiant, living, breathing color.

Nearly half a century later, I'm still appreciative for the gift those astronauts, those three wise men, provided in choosing to read from Genesis on Christmas Eve. I'm also grateful for my son's gift in sharing his rapture in watching that astonishing historic scene. What a heavenly night indeed.

~ *Terri Elders*

Enter the Cow

One of the proudest moments for a parent is the debut performance of their little bundle of joy in the church Christmas play. Sometimes that joyous moment can also be their most embarrassing.

I was working at our church in Ft. Lauderdale, Forida as administrative assistant to our music minister. We were particularly excited that year as our focus was going to be on the children's production for the holidays. We had a large group of kids involved, who were working hard and excited about the musical. A nativity scene would be the perfect ending, and we discussed using a few live animals.

"Hey!" I had an epiphany. "Why don't we use a few of the younger kids to dress up as animals for the nativity?"

"Yes!" "Great idea!" Everyone agreed.

I was thrilled because my little three-year-old darling had just dressed as Floyd the Cow at our harvest festival. I quickly volunteered him to play the cow part, and we chose a precious little girl for our lamb.

We decided it would be best to have adults on the platform with the little ones, so I was assigned to be Mary, one of the fathers to be Joseph, and our little lamb's mom would be an angel. It was going to be delightful. We knew our congregation would love it!

The nativity scene characters only needed to be present for the final dress rehearsal. The nativity scene had been built on a platform that was placed over the baptistery where the curtain could be opened by remote control.

That was the perfect place for it except for one thing: The edge of the platform had no barrier and was a straight drop down five feet into the choir loft. As parents, we were concerned about this, but we talked to our budding little thespians about staying in place and being very, very quiet during the song. We were set, this was going to be the best Christmas production our kids had ever done. After much cheering, laughing, and merriment, we all held hands and ended the final rehearsal with prayer.

The next morning I was so excited to get my little one into his cow costume! Maybe I should have said no when he insisted on wearing the cowbell, but doggone, he was just so cute, I couldn't resist that precious expectant face. He promised to keep it still, so I let him wear it.

The fact that I was talking to a three-year-old didn't give me pause at the time.

We arrived at church early for a quick run-through and could feel the excitement. The lights were just right, the sound guy, who was my husband, was perfect. The characters knew their lines, and the singing was amazing. Our little stable animals were beyond adorable in their costumes.

What could possibly go wrong?

Since our animal scene was at the end of the musical, we stayed in the back, keeping the little ones settled and ready to go on stage. We could hear the congregation laughing in the right places, and applauding at exceptional moments. Finally, we took our places on the nativity platform, feeling the emotion at the retelling of our Savior's birth. The young boy performing the solo was singing beautifully as the curtain began opening to reveal the nativity scene. There was a reverent hush over the congregation. That was a Holy Ground moment.

Enter the cow!

It started with a soft, protracted "Mooooo." Surprised, my worshipful prayer became a firm, yet gentle, "Shhh!" This nonetheless, did not stop the mooing, which began to include a little hop. My firm, yet still gentle, "shhh," this time included "The Look." You know the one. It's the one that says, "Stop that and stop it now!"

However, the excitement of a three-year-old dressed in a cow costume complete with a cowbell, on stage in the Christmas play was more than my little angel could handle. His hopping and mooing got louder, and he started waving.

Before I could even breathe the prayer, *not the bell, please not the bell,* I heard that cowbell clanging. I could see Joseph and our mom-angel trying not to laugh.

Suddenly, my mooing, hopping, and clanging little cow took off running around the manger. I can't say how the real mother of our Lord might have handled that in the stable, but this mother franticly reached behind her to grab this out-of-control-cow.

Now, this was no Ferdinand, content to sit in the pasture and sniff flowers, but a hyped up, determined little calf that pulled out of my grasp and kept going. As a mom, I knew the edge of the platform was a concern. The only thing I could grab next was his cow tail as he plowed around me. I wanted to stay in character, truly I did, but I saw no way to stop the madness. So this Mary tackled him, right there in the stable, and marched him back to his place behind the manger. As the curtain began to close, I breathed a sigh of relief while he continued to moo and wave.

My little calf performed in many church productions as he grew into the Godly man he is today. My son and I have written many scripts together for church plays over the years, but I still like to tease him about his debut as the cow. He is always quick to remind me, "Well Mom, at least you've never had to chase me around the manger again!"

No, but that might be because I keep his cowbell locked up!

~ Janet Bryant Campbell

23

No Room in the Sky

Thursday prior to Christmas Day, my family (wife Sherry, two children, and Leaderdog Zoey) had plans to visit Sherry's family in north central Wisconsin. Although driving through a wintry mix, we reached the airport in plenty of time to check in and board our flight.

After arriving at Gate 22, we settled into seats to await the announcement to board. Minutes later, we heard, "Ladies and gentlemen." Our conversation halted. An airport official continued over the terminal public address system. "We regret to inform you that your flight from Detroit Metro Airport to Mosinee-Central Wisconsin Airport has been cancelled. A bus will meet you outside your designated gate area for ground transportation."

A snowstorm was affecting airport runways in suburban Detroit, Chicago, Greenbay, and the Mosinee-Central Wisconsin Airport where we were to land.

Smiles from patrons turned to frowns and grimaces over the sudden change in transport mode. The words of a song played in the background, "Do you hear what I hear?" Patrons sharing the gate area surely heard.

Joy deflated upon hearing the public announcement.

They began to mumble.

"We better get a refund back for this."

"Can you contact the family and let them know we're going by bus?"

"I had plans to give my fiancée an engagement ring over dinner this evening."

"I'm glad we sent the gifts ahead of time."

More words of the song again. "Do you see what I see? A star. A star."

I reflected on our moment and that all one could see up there was a sky full of snow and storms. There was no room in that sky for an airplane.

Within a half-hour the Greyhound bus filled with passengers and luggage en route to points in Wisconsin. We could expect a 10-to-12 hour drive overnight, with rest stops along the way. I had Leaderdog Zoey lie by my seat and said a silent prayer that this venture would have a minimal amount of problems.

During the night, I again thought of there being no room in the sky, which led me to thinking about a stressed-out innkeeper in a little Judean town telling a young woman and her husband there was no room in the inn. My family's bus ride instead of an airline flight had no comparison to that couple delivering a baby in a stable instead of a comfortable inn.

Shortly after 9:00 a.m. the bus pulled into the airport at Mosinee. My wife's parents had arrived to pick us up. Their Town and Country van had the familiar aroma of popcorn and snack food as we climbed in to complete the remaining miles of the journey.

We observed Christmas on Saturday with my brother-in-law's family, two sons and his wife. Earlier, names had been exchanged for gift giving. The family gathered in the basement and took turns opening presents. The weekend time included sledding, occasional winter walks, plenty of feasting, attending Christmas Eve services, playing games of Uno, and watching a televised Packers football game. We were able to fly back to Michigan as scheduled.

That trip was a wonderful gift to us. We cherished those memories, but later, with a family to raise, work, demands on our lives, and limited finances, we wondered if our combined income would be enough to pay the airline fare to go to my sister's wedding.

Then another gift arrived, unexpected. The mail brought a voucher from the airline. I told Sherry, "We can use this toward paying the fare to the wedding."

"Wow," she exclaimed. "God really does work in mysterious ways."

I smiled and agreed as she added, "At Christmastime, we celebrate the Savior coming to our world and giving us good things. But good things happen throughout the year and on his timetable."

"You're right, honey," I said. "This is just another Christmas moment."

Then I remembered our Christmas when there was no room in the sky, and the first Christmas when there was no room in the inn. But God knows what we might consider an inconvenience or something negative can result in something good or even the most wonderful gift the world could ever know.

~ David Russell

24

Gingerbread House

The Christmas tree sparkled with tiny tea lights. The fireplace crackled with warmth. The kitchen smelled yummy from the sweet fragrance of cinnamon on baked goods. Grandpa and Uncle Greg watched television in the living room. Uncle Greg sat on the floor with his legs extended. In the kitchen, I the grandmother, gathered the candies and cookies needed to construct and decorate a gingerbread house. I had the job of being Chief Clean-up Officer for the family's Christmas Gingerbread decorating party. I loved seeing the interaction between my 25-year-old daughter and her young children as they continue the tradition started many years ago.

Frank, the three-year-old asked, "Mom, what's a gingerbread house?" Without giving her a chance to explain, he said, "Can I have a candy cane?"

As his mom opened the graham cracker box, she responded to his first question. "We're going to build a house from graham crackers held together with frosting. Then, we will decorate the house with candy. That's the fun part. After the house is decorated, we can take pieces of candy off the house and eat them. Building the house is something we do every Christmas."

Frank joined his five-year-old sister, Austin, at the dining room table and awaited their mom's instructions.

Mom entered the dining room with a cookie sheet lined with tin foil. She sat the cookie sheet on the table between Frank and Austin.

"Can I have a candy cane? I want a candy cane," Frank said.

"Frank! Just wait a minute!" his mom said.

Unable to wait, he reached over her arm for a candy cane and knocked over one of the candy bowls, spilling the contents onto the cookie sheet.

Frank did not get his candy cane.

Mom set down several bowls filled with gumdrops, peppermint spin wheels, tiny marshmallows, pretzel sticks, Red Hots, Life Savers, and candy canes. She pulled up a chair and sat between the two children. Holding up two graham crackers she began her instruction. "Take a section of cracker and hold it upright, like this." She showed each of the children how to hold their graham cracker.

The children followed their mom's directions. She used a spoon to push white icing into a cake decorator pump and set the spoon on the table.

"Grab your graham cracker and hold it like I showed you."

Both children complied.

Mom filled the seams with frosting where the crackers met. When the first crackers were seamed together, the children added cracker after cracker and built four walls and a roof.

After the walls and roof were anchored, the fun began.

Austin wanted to construct windows on three sides of the house and a front door. She used icing to anchor the salted pretzel sticks and one-fourth of a black gumdrop for a doorknob.

Mom frosted one side of the house so she and Frank could make a chimney. "Right here, Frank," she said, "Put these Red Hots on the wall where I put the frosting."

Frank placed the bowl of Red Hots right in front him. At the same time, unable to resist, his little fingers stuck several into his mouth. Just as quickly, he tried to spit them out and started to cry, "Mommy, Mommy!"

Mom picked him up and carried him to the kitchen trash can, had him spit them out, and returned him to the table. She gave him water to cool his mouth.

Despite the excitement, Austin finished her windows

"I don't want to do this anymore," Frank said. He left the dining room and sat down by Uncle Greg on the floor.

Mom helped Austin anchor shredded wheat squares on the roof. Then she gathered a few ice cream cones, saying, "If we turn them upside down, they will look like Christmas trees." **She** dripped several drops of green food coloring into the bowl and whipped it. When she finished, Austin said, "I want to lick the beater."

Frank jumped up and ran to the dining room. "I want a beater too."

With a butter knife, Austin put green frosting on the ice cream cones, and on her hands. When finished, she anchored the trees to the cookie sheet, and decorated the green trees with Red Hots.

"Oh, the gingerbread house is so beautiful!" said Austin.

Frank, too, was impressed. "Can we take the house to show Grandpa?"

"Sure, but wait for one minute so I can help you."

Mom said to Uncle Greg, who sat on the floor between the dining room and the living room, "Greg, don't move."

Mom placed the cookie sheet in Austin's and Frank's hands, and cautioned, "Frank, go slow."

With every step they placed one foot in front of the other. Austin planned to step over Uncle Greg's long legs, stretched out on the floor. As the children started to step over his stretched out legs, Greg pulled them to his chest. His movement startled Austin, caught her off balance, and down she and Frank went. They landed on top of the gingerbread house.

Talk about a mess, all over their faces and clothes!

The trauma was painful. The tears flowed. Austin and Frank must have cried ten buckets full of tears. Poor Uncle Greg was horrified.

The next day, Uncle Greg went to the market and visited the bakery department. There he found a decorated gingerbread house. He purchased it and brought it home to his niece and nephew. They were elated.

Austin said, "Now we have a beautiful gingerbread house and we can eat some candy off of it."

Finally, Mom answered the second question Frank had asked the day before. He was perfectly content when his request was granted after saying, "Can I have a candy cane?"

As a mother, grandmother, and now great-grandmother, my blessing is the bond that was built between the three generations from the decorating party. Photos and stories will linger. Remembering the seasonal joy of the evening will bring laughter. Those are the family ties that last.

~ *Gayle Fraser*

Dandy-Walker Christmas

My instincts told me, after 17 years of marriage, 2013 would be our last Christmas together in our home. I didn't know how I was going to pull it off, but I was determined to celebrate as usual.

Eight months earlier, after several years of pushing doctors for an answer to the declining physical condition of my husband, Douglas, he was diagnosed with Dandy-Walker Syndrome.

All the pieces had been there, but it was only when a skilled neurosurgeon spent time with Doug's medical records and saw "malignant melanoma," the newest addition to his list of medical conditions, that the puzzle came together and showed the rare Dandy-Walker configuration.

Doug was unable to walk, or feed and dress himself. Sometimes he fell multiple times a day. With little control over his bladder, he had me get him up every 10 to 12 minutes during the night to take him to the bathroom. I dared not take my eyes off of him for even a few minutes. If I left his sight he had panic attacks. I hired a caregiver for one day a week so I could take care of family and personal business. The caregivers could not manage his care. I became sleep deprived and desperate.

The solution to Dandy-Walker Syndrome is placement of a permanent programmable shunt into the brain to drain the water that accumulates in a ventricle of the brain and transport the fluid to the abdominal cavity. Since Dandy-Walker is typically diagnosed in children the shunt is usually inserted in a pediatric brain. Doug, however, was 63 years old. The surgeons refused to consider placing a shunt in his brain and change its configuration after so many years.

Near Christmastime, I knew we couldn't continue like that. The fire department would not keep coming and picking Doug up off the floor. I needed to sleep and to stop nodding off while driving Doug to doctor's appointments. I was afraid I would get hurt lifting Doug and his wheelchair in and out of the house, maneuvering it through our non-ADA-modified home. Doug didn't want to go to a skilled nursing facility. I wanted to honor his wishes. I also wanted what was best for him. If we could have one last Christmas together as a family in our own home, I would face the decisions about our future.

My daughter Tina, son-in-law Hank, and son Kurtis arrived on Christmas Eve. They found me in tears, the house a mess and the artificial tree in its bag. Unwrapped gifts sat in the middle of the living room floor. The groceries I purchased at 2:00 a.m. while maneuvering Doug in the battery- powered shopping cart were still in bags on the kitchen counter.

Doug and I had always taken communion at our church's Christmas Eve candlelight service. We wanted to go — one last time. With the family's help, Doug and I were able to feel blessed at that service.

After church, we returned to what was becoming like a different house. Presents had been wrapped, potatoes peeled, table set, floors swept, bedding changed…and they'd found Christmas decorations that gave a festive look.

On Christmas morning, we began to open gifts. After opening one gift, Doug needed to lie down. We related as a family while waiting for Doug to be rested enough for gift opening. It took all day. Still, no one complained. At the end of the day, I received from Tina, a massage therapist, one of my best presents as her capable hands soothed my tired muscles and gave me needed rest.

The following morning I walked to Tina and Hank's car as they prepared to return home, 300 miles away. I looked around, surprised. The bushes that had grown over the sidewalk, often entangling the wheels and handles of Doug's chair, had been trimmed. Shrubbery had been removed so I could take the trash and recycling carts in and out with ease. The porch had been swept clean of the fall leaves blown in by the winter storms. The driveway and walkways appeared to have been pressure washed. The grass and weeds that had grown in the cracks were gone. The box of leftover plumbing parts sitting by the garage door had been moved.

I don't know when my children did all that. They gave me and Doug that last Christmas together and more.

In 2014 Doug was in hospice at Christmastime. He passed away in January 2015.

I do not remember what wrapped presents my family gave me for Christmas in 2013, but I will forever remember their gifts of compassion, mercy, kindness, patience, hope and love.

~ Karen R. Hessen

26

Where Is the Merry in Christmas?

Rehab center, jail, and illness assault my waking mind. I throw off the covers, put my feet on the floor, close my eyes, and take a deep breath. I trudge into the living room where a Christmas tree, gifts, and stockings greet my eyes. I can't wrap my mind around the extremes of Merry Christmas and the despondency I feel in my heart.

An epidemic of anxiety, fear, and grief has spread through my family. My litany of sorrows is mind-numbing — my daughter in rehab, my eight-year-old granddaughter wondering why Mommy won't be home for Christmas, my brother in jail, my sister's brush with death from an unknown illness that lingers. Each of these maladies alone could paralyze a family, and each of these situations is so foreign that my family never dreamed of experiencing any of them.

Where is the hope, the peace, the joy, of the season?

I pour a cup of coffee, sit down on the couch, and my eyes lock on the Advent wreath adorning the coffee table. The words of the prophet Isaiah come to mind. They were repeated by Jesus when he said, "The Spirit of the Lord is on me, because he has anointed me to proclaim good news to the poor. He has sent me to proclaim freedom for the prisoners and recovery of sight for the blind, to set the oppressed free..." (Luke 4:18 NLT)

I gaze at the Advent candles representing Hope, Love, Peace and Joy, and feel Christ's peace gently infuse my spirit.

I know the Lord is Hope. I know he is Love. I've experienced his Peace. When I focus on him instead of my circumstances, I feel the constant Joy he gives me, even in difficult circumstances.

My gaze returns to the Christmas tree and the twinkling star on top, the brightly wrapped gifts bought with love, and the mantle. Hanging there are festive stockings bearing the names of those closest to my heart. The despondency that engulfed me only moments before dissipates.

I've found the Merry in Christmas, even Christmas this year. The Merry in Christmas is Christ.

~ Susan Dollyhigh

27

Baking Up a Little Love, Joy, and Hope

After 17 years in Christian ministry I was burnt out.
Toast.
Deep fried.

The demands of ministry had been buried under even heavier personal stressors. Within three years I had sent my younger son off to U.S. Army boot camp; nursed my father through a year of cancer, then held his hand as he went to heaven; nursed my older son through cancer and then watched helplessly as he turned his back on the Lord. I had relocated, changed jobs, and endured an ugly church split which resulted in the loss of many dear friends.

I was physically, mentally, emotionally and spiritually exhausted. So, from 1990 to1993, I left the ministry and worked a boring, non-creative job as an inventory clerk in a warehouse. My workdays were filled with tracking ba-zillions of numbers that gave me an equal number of headaches. But that boredom gave my spirit opportunity to heal, to recover, and to begin growing again. The salary was small but my family and I were able to survive by stretching every penny to its maximum, and by watching God provide for us in unexpected ways.

In 1992, I agreed to co-teach a small women's Sunday school class in my church. Those ladies were a great joy to me and I relished every minute of preparing and teaching the Bible lessons. My mind perked up with the stimulation. My heart began to crawl out of the pain into God's embrace. I again sensed the joy of his presence in my quiet times.

As Christmas 1992, drew near I thought about how much I enjoyed baking and making candies and elaborate treats for the holidays. I had an arsenal of favorite recipes from friends and family. But that Christmas I knew there would be no special treats at our house. We would be doing good to have a Christmas turkey on our table. But I was a good little soldier, so I sucked it up and thanked God for the huge supply of venison that had been given to us by my boss. I was getting good at disguising venison in 100 different ways.

And I tried to convince myself that I didn't really have time to do a lot of fancy baking anyway.

The Sunday morning before Thanksgiving I pulled into a parking space at church, grabbed my bags and my daughter, and ran for the children's building. I kissed Tabitha on the cheek and made my way to my Sunday school classroom in record time. I was armed with my Bible and yet another exciting object lesson for my class.

When I opened the door the room was totally dark. Hmm...unusual. Where was everybody? I groped for the light switch. Click! I was shocked by a loud, "Surprise!" The ladies of my class jumped out of their seats like cheerleaders at conference play-offs.

They all yelled, "Happy Thanksgiving!" and "Merry Christmas!" One friend took my tote bag, another slid my coat off my shoulders, a third friend took my purse. My co-teacher ushered me to the front of the room. Resting on top of a lacy tablecloth was a Christmas platter loaded with cookies, a crystal bowl filled with punch and a humongous wicker basket overflowing with baking supplies.

I was speechless.

"Go ahead, take a look!" somebody said. I rummaged through the basket and found every form of chocolate imaginable, icings, cake mixes, nuts, coconut, three kinds of sugar, flour, vanilla, cinnamon, raisins, honey, corn syrup, condensed milk... everything I needed to make my visions of sugar plums become Christmas realities.

Everything I needed to keep me baking for a long, long time.

I picked through the boxes, bags and cans and I cried. I sniffed. I blubbered.

One sweet lady handed me tissues. Another placed a pile of greeting cards on my lap. "Open them! Quick!" she said. "We only have an hour until worship service begins."

I sniffed and blew my nose, then started ripping into the envelopes. Money slid out of every card. $5, $10, $20 fell into my lap. I cried some more. It was humbling and oh, so wonderful to feel the love that every card, every dollar, every baking ingredient brought. With each card I received a hug from the signer of that card, and it felt so inexplicably good. It had been a long time since I had been able to feel such overwhelming love.

Everyone chattered, laughed and ate cookies. We sang Christmas carols. Then my sweet friends wrapped up the leftover cookies and carried them and the basket out to my car. They poked all of the cards and money into a brown envelope and stuffed it into my tote bag.

"The money is for milk and eggs and whatever else you need. Now you can bake 'til your heart's content," my co-teacher said as she gave me one more squeeze.

I cried all the way through worship service.

Those were not sad tears dripping off my chin. They were tears of joy. My dear friends had given me much more than sugar and spices that morning. More than love, too. They had given me hope for tomorrow. Hope that our situation would get better, and that God would continue to provide for us until it did.

Isn't this the message and spirit of Christmas? Love. Joy. Hope.

God's Love wrapped in the flesh of a pauper's babe.

Joy in that same infant Savior who came to forgive us of our sins.

Hope for now and eternity, sleeping in the straw.

That basket of baking goodies gave me a tangible reminder of Jesus' love, joy and hope poured out on me through my friends. Love, joy and hope that could meet my every need — at Christmas and every day of every year to come.

~ Jean Matthew Hall

Unwrapping the Best First

A s a young child, I looked at the presents piled beneath the decorated tree. I had already found the packages with my name and shaken them while my parents were in the barn milking cows. Now it was finally Christmas Eve, and I could open my gifts. But I didn't realize then that sometimes the best gifts are not found under the tree. You discover them later. And that's how it was with a simple tradition my father began decades ago that has continued for generations.

Before we opened our wrapped gifts, Dad would gather our family around the tinseled tree and read aloud the story of Jesus' birth. Dad wanted us to focus on the real Gift of Christmas first. So he opened his black Bible and read with his strong German accent from Luke 2:8–20 KJV:

> There were in the same country shepherds abiding in the field, keeping watch over their flock by night. And, lo, the angel of the Lord came upon them, and the glory of the Lord shone round about them: and they were sore afraid.
>
> And the angel said unto them, "Fear not: for, behold, I bring you good tidings of great joy, which shall be to all people. For unto you is born this day in the city of David a Saviour, which is Christ the Lord. And this shall be a sign unto you; Ye shall find the babe wrapped in swaddling clothes, lying in a manger."
>
> And suddenly there was with the angel a multitude of the heavenly host praising God, and saying, "Glory to God in the highest, and on earth peace, good will toward men."
>
> And it came to pass, as the angels were gone away from them into heaven, the shepherds said one to another, "Let us now go even unto Bethlehem, and see this thing which is come to pass, which the Lord hath made known unto us."
>
> And they came with haste, and found Mary, and Joseph, and the babe lying in a manger. And when they had seen it, they made known abroad the saying which was told them concerning this child. And all they that heard it wondered at those things which were told them by the shepherds.

But Mary kept all these things, and pondered them in her heart.

And the shepherds returned, glorifying and praising God for all the things that they had heard and seen, as it was told unto them.

I can't say that I listened to each word or that my mind focused only on the story and not on the shiny wrapped packages. But I did realize that Jesus was the real reason why we celebrated Christmas.

The story made an impact, and over the years, the words became familiar and treasured. So it's not surprising that after my husband and I were married, we wanted to continue the Christmas-story tradition. Whether we opened our gifts on Christmas Eve or on Christmas Day, we read Luke's story first.

After two little ones were born into our family, we looked for creative ways to make the story interesting and age appropriate for them. When they were young, we read about Jesus' birth from a children's storybook with lots of pictures. I also saved Christmas cards with shepherds, wise men, angels, and Jesus in the manger and attached them to a wide ribbon to help tell the story. Sometimes we brought the story to life with drama, and our children dressed up as Mary and Joseph.

We also looked for ways to share the story with others. One December, we invited our grade-school-aged neighbor children to our home for a party, and they tried on nativity costumes. The next evening their parents came for dessert. While one of the dads read the Christmas story from Luke, the children acted it out. It seemed a holy moment as the usually rambunctious kids, dressed as angels, shepherds, and wise men, bowed in worship by the homemade wooden manger holding a doll.

Other times, when we had guests in our home for a meal, we wrote verses from Luke 2 on slips of paper and put them inside place cards by our plates. Before eating our dessert, we took turns reading our verses from the Christmas story. To add fresh perspective to the well-known account, sometimes we used a different Bible version, switching from *King James Version* to the *New International Version* or *The Message*.

I remember one special Christmas Eve when our large extended family gathered in my sister's home in West Seattle. On the way over, we stopped at the retirement center to pick up my parents, then in their late eighties. To my surprise, they carried armloads of gifts. After dinner, even though my father was eager to give us the gifts, he still read the Christmas story first. Then my parents handed each of us a wrapped package with the same present inside — a treasured book that Dad had written about their escape from Russia and God's faithfulness in their lives.

My parents are in heaven, but Dad's custom of opening the best first continues. Now with married children and grandchildren, we've adapted the Christmas-story tradition to suit them. Often I tell the story in a mixed-up way so the grandkids can correct me. To do this, I mount Christmas cards with pictures of the nativity story on chopsticks and print *stop* on the back of each card. Everyone gets a sign.

As I tell the story, the kids and adults hold up their "stop signs" whenever I say something incorrectly. For example, I begin, "Once upon a time," and they stop me since this isn't a fairy tale. I continue with wrong details, such as, "Mary and Joseph traveled by airplane to Seattle." The grandkids listen carefully to catch mistakes and laugh when I make them.

Last year our teenaged grandson read the story from the Bible and embellished it, while the rest of us held up our "stop" signs and corrected the story. Before we knew it, we had unwrapped the greatest Gift and were ready to open our own packages.

I'm grateful my father started the custom of reading the Christmas story before we opened our presents. As a child, I found it hard to wait. But now I appreciate the gift he gave us. It's a legacy we are passing on to our children and grandchildren, because Jesus' birth will always be the best Gift for all generations — both now and for eternity.

Thanks be to God for his indescribable gift!
2 Corinthians 9:15 NIV

~ *Lydia E. Harris*

29

Christmas Nostalgia

It happens every Christmas.

I get nostalgic.

Perhaps it's the music…

Whenever those old familiar carols play, sweet memories come flooding over me, like the year that my family decided to surprise Grams and Gramps in Pennsylvania with an unexpected Christmas visit.

I remember it like it was yesterday. Scurrying around the house like Christmas mice in the darkness of the early morning hours, packing the car with gifts, travel games and suitcases. It was such delicious fun!

When the long stretches through Indiana and Ohio began to curb even a child's enthusiasm, we broke the monotony by singing. Dad taught us how to harmonize so we could sing in four parts. Sis sang the melody, I sang alto, Mom baritone and Dad sang bass. It was amazing how fast time flew by singing every Christmas carol and jingle we could think of!

By the time we reached the Pennsylvania border, snow was falling. Heavily. Snowflakes as big as quarters fell from the sky. The tree branches were laden with snow, creating white arches over the road for us to pass under. I was sure we had entered Winter Wonderland.

When we reached my grandparents house, we tiptoed as quietly as we could up to the front door and began singing the Christmas songs we had practiced over the many miles. As soon as Gramps heard us, he made a beeline for the kitchen to load up a plate of Christmas goodies and opened the door fully expecting to see the neighbors out caroling.

I can still see the look on his face. Tears shimmered in his eyes, and in our eyes too.

Whenever I hear those old familiar carols play, my mind wanders back to Winter Wonderland, to Pennsylvania, to the look on my sweet grandpa's face. Tears again shimmer in my eyes.

Perhaps it is the music…

But, then again, it might be the scent of Christmas cookies wafting in the air.

Just one whiff of Christmas cookies in the oven triggers memories of days long past when Mom, Sis and I used to whip up batches of cookies with hysterical giggling sprinkled in for good measure. Or the years spent in my mother-in-law's warm, cozy kitchen where a tradition of Christmas-cookie baking took root and continues still, though she now bakes cookies in heaven with Jesus.

Perhaps it is the scent of Christmas cookies...

Or maybe it's snow on the ground.

The first heavy snowfall of the season always transports me to back to Christmases spent sledding with my cousins, and my Grandma O. Sledding with my grandma was not for the faint of heart. She was full of shenanigans. One of her favorite ways to fly down a high hill was what she termed "sandwich-style," with her lying on her stomach on a toboggan with the rest of us cousins stacked on top. Shrieks of laughter filled the air as we whizzed our way to the bottom. Grandma O's shrieks were the loudest.

Maybe it is the snow on the ground...

Or maybe it's all that and something more.

I thank the sweet Savior for the precious gift of memories. For the ability to call to mind my loved ones' faces, to hear their laughter echo in my heart and know that some day we will enjoy each another's company again, with the scent of heaven heavy in the air and laughter resounding as we celebrate that precious reunion.

~ Julie Miller

30

Home for Christmas

The year was 2005. I was seven years old and about to spend my first Christmas in the mountains of western North Carolina. My mom, dad, brother, sister, and I had moved from Las Vegas, Nevada. I knew that this Christmas would be different from all the others since I was leaving the only home I knew.

Right away, Dad, who grew up in the mountains, decided to show us some of his "home." First thing, he said we had to get a tree. We couldn't get just any tree. We had to get the perfect tree. In Las Vegas, there weren't any trees. As far as the eye could see, there was desert.

So, you can imagine my reaction to seeing nothing but trees after moving here at a young and impressionable age. In Las Vegas my eyes could see infinity. Here, the view was blocked by mountains on all sides.

The day after Thanksgiving, we drove to a tree farm with the intention of getting a nice Christmas tree for our living room that had a cathedral ceiling.

We had looked around for a while, but Dad said we couldn't settle on just any tree, so we kept searching. The owner directed us to another section of the farm where the biggest trees grew. Finally, after what seemed like forever, we found it.

The tree stood almost three times taller than the average tree, measuring right at 14 feet tall. The trunk of the tree was thicker than all the trees in the farm. It was the perfect tree, and we all knew it. We bought it, tied it to the top of our huge suv, and drove it home to put in our living room.

The decorating was hard work, included a ladder, but the end result was quite satisfying, seeing that behemoth covered in colorful lights and ornaments.

Christmas was getting closer, and on Christmas Eve, my parents said we were going to the Biltmore Estate in Asheville. They were excited and I wondered if it was anything like the Strip, back home.

No! It was a mansion. Inside, lights twinkled everywhere you looked and decorations covered the walls. I'd thought our Christmas tree was the biggest in the world, so I was amazed to see theirs was twice the size of ours.

We began to walk through the many rooms. Although we had a fireplace in our house, this mansion had them in about every room. The light of the fires glowed softly as they warmed the rooms. I heard many different types of Christmas music. In one room, a violinist played a Christmas carol. In another, a group sang "White Christmas." I could hardly wait to see what would be in the next room.

Other people walking through the mansion talked quietly to each other about what we were seeing and hearing and where they came from. They had come from just about everywhere. They all seemed friendly and happy and full of joy. After leaving the mansion, we went to one of their fancy restaurants for dinner, and not the kind where you order hamburgers and French fries.

After dinner, Dad led us to a horse drawn carriage so we could ride on the estate grounds, through the snow. I'd heard about snow, but had never seen it. There were white patches along the trails. And no, it hadn't come up out of the ground. A couple months later I'd learn what it was like when it fell from the sky.

But on that ride, the winter wind chilled me. Blankets were in the carriage and we wrapped them around us. We were also provided with hot chocolate that warmed my throat and tasted good on that cold night. In Las Vegas we would have given visitors bottles of water to carry around because of the intense heat.

Later that night, Dad read about the birth of Jesus from the Bible, and made sure we knew about the real meaning of Christmas. Mom baked cookies and we watched Christmas movies.

That's the Christmas I remember as being the most impressive and making me feel like I was truly home.

Home for Christmas is being with family and having good times, whether in the desert or the mountains.

– Luke Lehman

31

A Christmas Feast

Christmas Eve came cold for Mrs. Cardinal. Snow had started early this year, and she didn't feel prepared for the long winter ahead. She had begged her husband to join their cousins who flew south each year, but he just shook his pretty red head and said, "We've survived many a winter in Ohio. We'll be fine."

But they weren't fine. The trees were icy and cold, and food was scarce. Many of their human friends were on vacation, and their bird feeders swung sadly empty. Mrs. Cardinal flew over a nearby hedge and checked the yard with the big brown feeder shaped like a mini human house. Her hopes were high. This was one of her favorite places to eat. The owner loved flowers, and each year the bird feeder was surrounded with blooms.

She didn't see any other birds nearby so she landed on the feeder, and eagerly looked inside. Only one sunflower seed remained. She reached and reached for it but couldn't get her beak far enough inside.

Chirping sadly, she flew to the nearby fir tree and wearily scanned the horizon for other feeding options. What would they do?

"Mommy?" A little human's voice caught her attention.

A child had stopped beneath the tree and was staring at her. Normally Mrs. Cardinal would flit away, but she was so tired.

"Yes?" The child's mother also paused and looked up at the tree.

"I think that bird is hungry."

"I'm sure it's fine Sweetie."

"No!" The child's voice was insistent. "Jesus told me, she's hungry. Can't we feed her?"

Her mother leaned down. "What do you mean, Jesus told you?"

"I listened in my heart like you said. Can't we help?"

"I don't know. I'm not sure we have any bird food." Her mother responded.

The child reached into her mother's purse and pulled out a small snack bag. "What about this?"

Mrs. Cardinal could hardly contain her excitement when the child dropped a pile of shelled sunflower seeds at the base of the tree.

"Here you go pretty bird!" The child called cheerily. "Merry Christmas!"

As soon as the humans were out of sight, Mrs. Cardinal dropped to the ground and chirped for her husband and their friends to join the feast.

As the little red birds flocked happily in the snow, eating the life-giving seeds, their Creator smiled. His heart was full of joy for the continued songs of his feathered friends, but most of all for the generous open heart of his little girl.

- Kristen Meyer Harmon

32

A Blizzard for Christmas

Christmas memories are plentiful in my heart and most are warm and cozy. Some are steeped in tradition and others wrapped in the scent of my mother's cookies baking or the Christmas turkey roasting. For the most part all are delightful except for the one little gray cloud that annually cast a shadow on the holiday festivities, although the event did not take place every year until our return to school after New Year's Day.

When I was in grade school it was often the custom, after Christmas vacation, for each child to stand and tell the class all about the most favorite treasure Santa delivered. The problem for me was that at our house Santa seemed to lean more toward necessary treasures rather than the frivolous Chatty Cathy, Easy Bake Oven, or GI Joe variety of goodies I saw splashed on the pages of the Sears Wish Book.

Santa always made sure I had a new coloring book and crayons, and a new board game to play. And every Christmas morning without fail my baby doll was decked out in a beautiful new outfit that Mom assured me Mrs. Claus designed and sewed by hand just for me. As far as I was concerned Christmas didn't get any better than that. The rest of the surprises under the tree usually took the form of mittens or socks or maybe a pair of corduroys or pajamas and slippers. All useful and practical gifts.

I kind of admired Santa for figuring out that it wasn't always easy for Mom and Dad to keep a family of seven afloat considering Mom stayed home to take care of us. If Santa's surprises seemed a bit more on the practical side at our house, that was just fine with me.

The trouble entered the picture when I had to stand up in class and broadcast what my favorite treasure was.

As much as I hate to admit it, I was always slightly embarrassed that the hand-made doll clothes that topped my list just didn't compare to the Jingle Jumps, Spirographs, and Etch-A-Sketch screens being touted by my classmates. So usually I just…lied. I'd pick a popular toy and brag all about it while praying to God that nobody would ask to come over to my house and play with it.

Real panic set in the year Miss Maxwell, my third grade teacher, announced that she wanted us to bring our favorite toy to class for Show and Tell. I started fretting the moment those words sailed to the back of the classroom and landed in my ever so paranoid ears. *Now what?*

It was the day before Christmas Eve. We sang Christmas carols and colored holiday pictures all afternoon. As a grand finale for the day, Miss Maxwell gave each of us a box, which she decorated with red and green ribbon that twirled into a huge curly bow in the center, filled with Christmas hard tack candy. There I was in the midst of a grade school Christmas blast-a-thon and all I could think about was the post Christmas show that, to me, was a disaster waiting to happen. I just didn't know how to make new pajamas and slippers or whatever Santa would bring me seem like a project the elves were working overtime to finish just so little Annie wouldn't be disappointed.

I left class that day with my brightly wrapped box of candy from Miss Maxwell in hand and my stomach in a knot. When I got home Mom was in the kitchen taking the umpteenth batch of Christmas cookies out of the oven. Right off the bat she said, "I bet you're excited that tomorrow is Christmas Eve."

I smiled.

She continued, "I have a feeling Santa has something very special in mind for you." I smiled again.

From your mouth to Santa's ear, I thought.

Christmas Eve day passed quickly as I helped Mother with last minute chores, getting ready for our Christmas dinner. But oh, how slowly Christmas Eve passes once you put out the snack for Santa and say goodnight.

I lay in my bunk bed wondering if Santa had some secret pact with Mom. Maybe she bribed him with a batch of her delicious cookies to find out what he was going to bring me. Maybe she has some inside information and there really was some fantastic Barbie Doll dream-come-true-toy in my future.

When morning came no one had to wake me. At the first sign of daylight I started poking at my sister and asking if she thought it was time to go downstairs. She didn't fool me. She was just as excited as I was.

Mom heard us, came into our room and gave us the green light. Mom led the way down the steps, and as usual I was the last in line behind my older brother and sisters. When I finally made my way over to the tree I could hardly believe my eyes. There before me stood the tallest, fattest, whitest, teddy bear I had ever seen in all my eight years of living. And there around its neck was one huge red satin ribbon tied in a bow with a note on it that said, "To Annie, from Santa."

I knelt down in front of it and touched his snowy white plush fur and his red felt tongue just to make sure he was real. Then I threw my arms around his neck and kissed his fuzzy cheek.

My Dad, laughed and said, "That teddy bear is twice as tall as you are, Annie!"

Right he was about that. One look convinced me that an entire team of elves must have been working on this teddy every day since the day after Christmas last year just to finish him in time.

Show and Tell here I come!

In fact, I could hardly wait. My new teddy bear, Blizzard, might not be pictured on the pages of the Sears Wish Book but he was bound to make a big splash at Show and Tell by virtue of his size alone. And that he did.

Blizzard was a hit to everyone he met that day, with the exception of my older sister Marie, who was charged with the chore of dragging him to school in my mother's folding shopping cart. She was in the fifth grade then. I don't think she's ever recovered from the humiliation of it. Apparently giant teddy bears don't hold the same mystique for fifth graders as they do for third graders.

Years later, I learned the story behind my Christmas gift. Blizzard had been a supermarket display bear for a Snow Crop brand orange juice promotion. The company mascot/logo was a big white bear. When the supermarket was taking down the display, they were going to throw the bear in the trash, and my Mom asked if she could have it.

For this third grader, Blizzard was a Christmas Show and Tell dream come true.

~ Annmarie B. Tait

Meltdown at
the Customer Service Desk

I don't know what came over me, but it wasn't pretty. I'm normally very even-tempered, but not this afternoon. I had just spent a torturous half hour waiting in line at the post office, and now I was waiting again — this time behind a woman in the customer service line at Target.

All I had to do was return two belts. I admit it. I was already grumpy because I had to return the belts in the first place. I don't enjoy shopping, but I had braved the Black Friday sales the weekend before to snag some great clothing deals for my husband.

When the time came to choose belts to go with the outfits, I knew I was out of my league. Like a man trying to choose a woman's purse, I needed further insight. A quick phone call to my husband would solve the mystery. Unfortunately, my husband, who usually wears his phone on his hip, had chosen to take it off and lie down for a nap. When I couldn't reach him, I chose two belts I thought would work. Of course, they were the wrong size, the wrong style, and the wrong material.

So. two days later I'd not only shopped, but was now un-shopping. If there's one thing I hate more than shopping, it's un-shopping. And then shopping again for the same items.

Back to Target I'd gone. I had the belts, with the tags still on them, and the receipt. It should have been a simple transaction, right?

Until Frozen woman got between me and my refund.

Did you know, when you order a Ship-to-Store life-sized *Frozen* Elsa Doll, you cannot simply pick it up at the Customer Service desk? Apparently it requires the assistance of no fewer than three associates, including the one assigned to handle simple returns.

Like Secret Service agents preparing for a presidential visit to a foreign land, men with walkie-talkies and silicone earpieces direct traffic and ensure safe passage of Queen Elsa from the stockroom to the door. Small children holding tightly to their mothers' hands stop to wave as she passes by. All forward motion in the store grinds to a halt until the queen, surrounded by her entourage and safely ensconced in her red shopping cart limo, rolls out the door.

And all I wanted to do was to return two stinkin' belts.

When the customer service associate finally returned to her register, I plastered on a smile that convinced no one.

Mentally calculating the level of traffic that had exponentially increased between me and my destination during the 20-minute Elsa motorcade, I'd crossed off the errand I hoped to do enroute. I was stuffing down impatience and frustration while the lyrics from "Silent Night" mocked me in the background. "All is calm. All is bright...."

The only thing calm, I thought, *is Elsa, safe inside her nice dark box and on her way to her destination, which is more than I can say for myself.*

I'm not sure how the celebration of the birth of Christ becomes a season that brings out the worst in us, but it happens every year. In the hours that followed my near meltdown, I gained some perspective I think is worth sharing.

We can view challenging encounters like my Target stop in the same way. Every morning, even before we climb out of bed, we can say, "Today is a test, allowed by God, to give me the opportunity to show Jesus to someone. Will I pass or fail?"

Then, instead of being surprised by the fiery trial, we can expect it. Like a scheduled exam instead of a pop quiz, we are better prepared to pass if we know the test is coming.

It shouldn't surprise us that Christmas, the celebration of Christ's advent on the earth, brings out the worst in the world. Road rage, Black Friday stampedes, and increased numbers of robberies and purse snatchings are just a few examples of the sinful behavior we see during the holiday season.

In a strange way, even this points to Jesus.

Christ came into the world to save mankind from our sins. Because we can never be good enough (believe me, I tried really hard that day in Target), we all need a Savior. No amount of self-control or determination can make us perfect, yet perfect is God's standard if we want a relationship with him.

The sinful behavior we witness and exhibit during the holiday season is undeniable proof that we need the Christ of Christmas to transform us. Without the Holy Spirit living inside us, sanding off the rough spots in our character, and transforming us to be like Christ, we are hopeless.

So the next time Elsa rolls by you and you're about to have a meltdown, take a deep breath and remind yourself: This is a test — a test I can pass with Jesus' help.

And the next time you see someone in the middle of a meltdown, pray for her. Realize, this is why Jesus came — because sinners need a Savior. Then do what you can to breathe grace into the situation.

May God fill your holiday season with opportunities to shine for him.

~ Lori Hatcher

Barnyard Christmas Eve

She gave birth to her firstborn son; and she wrapped Him in cloths and
laid Him in a manger, because there was no room for them in the inn.

Luke 2:7 NAS

One Christmas Eve, after waving good-bye to our guests, I went to feed
and bed down my bunnies for the cold night. Grabbing some apple
slices as a treat for them I realized to my dismay, that in all the holiday rush,
fresh hay had been forgotten. Immediately my thoughts went to the farm
lady nearby. She loved animals too and would understand.

Quickly calling her, I apologized for the interruption. She seemed genuinely
glad to help. I wrapped a box of homemade cookies and hurried out the door.

From the hill, a stunning sunset showcased her farm. Pausing to take in
the brilliant orange and violet swirls, I realized this was a special moment,
compliments of the Father. In quiet adoration I took a moment to praise Him
for the gift of His Son.

Walking the darkened dirt path to the barnyard another surprise waited.
Ever so softly, from a speaker mounted nearby, sweet carols were drifting on
the hay and animal-scented air. Cows lowed quietly. A warm glow beckoned
from an opened door. In awe, I tiptoed closer. I thanked God for a tiny
glimpse into the wonder of that holy night when Jesus was born. Treading
silently, tears in my eyes, I stepped into the warm light anticipating a baby
in the manger.

Instead, there was my friend, greeting me with a big smile. "Perfect," she
said, "I had one bale of clover left! It's my Christmas gift to your bunnies!"

Handing her the cookies, I smiled and treasured the gift I had already
received so many years ago, far away in a manger.

Father, thank You for the most perfect gift of Your Son!

~ Bonnie Mae Evans

It Wouldn't Be Christmas Without Them

Momma and I were baking an imaginary cake in the kindergarten Sunday school's pint-sized kitchen when Daddy and the boys poked their heads in. "Ready?" Daddy asked with a grin.

Momma replied with a little let's-get-outa-here jig. Soon we were back in the car, skipping out on big people's church to go on a family adventure. We stopped at home just long enough to put on our play clothes, then drove to the grove of pecan trees north of town.

Our Chevy cruised along the November countryside. In the distance, trees appeared to dance in the crisp autumn breeze. They were like ancient giants with their arms flung high overhead, so high it looked as if they could touch the sky. When we arrived, their long swaying branches greeted us with a deafening silence.

There was a shiver in the air, and we saw our breath as we got out of the car. Daddy got the floppy old quilt from the trunk and spread it out on the ground. "Now, I'm gonna climb up there and shake 'em down. Stand clear."

Up he went — higher and higher until he reached what he thought was the perfect point. Then, he leaned down and started to jiggle the branches, gently at first, then harder and harder, until at last the nuts broke free and hailed down onto the old quilt.

As the storm of pecans showered before us, Bob, Bill and I scampered around, flipping the strays onto the quilt. All the while, I imagined all the cookies and candies that would soon find their way around them, not to mention the pecan pie that would provide a spectacular finale for our Thanksgiving and Christmas dinners.

We brought the lumpy quilt home, dumped the huge pile of nuts in the carport, bagged our treasure in brown paper bags, and hauled them into the furnace room to dry.

The next step was the cracking. Momma had invented a sure-fire procedure. She clamped the nutcracker onto the kitchen stool and placed a Sara Lee fruitcake tin underneath. How perfectly it caught the nuts as they fell open!

Crack, crunch, crack, drop. Crack, squash, crack, crack. Momma's rhythm was steady. As the pecans piled up, the goodness of the meat peeked out. Momma smiled as she concentrated on her task.

Silence. Oh boy, I knew what that meant!

Rattle time!

Momma put the lid on the Sara Lee tin, slid it off the stool into my waiting hands, and I shook that thing like it was the best maraca this side of Rio.

See, Momma had a theory. She said, "Pecans like being out of their shells, so if you crack them open enough and shake them in a tin hard enough, most of the time the outer covering simply falls off." Maybe that was her way of making the next task appear a bit easier. Her words certainly made it more exotic. And at age five, already possessing a bent for drama, exotic was very appealing to me.

As the official pecan sheller in our family, my job was to prepare the nuts for their ready-to-eat state. That meant picking out all the tiny particles of shell that didn't come off during my Carmen Miranda routine. It was a painstaking process that wore on what little patience I had.

Sitting at the kitchen table, my small fingers dusted the surface. Then, I used a metal pick to get down into the grooves of each pecan. The repetition helped me perfect my movements, as hundreds of pecans passed through my fingers.

Of course, some nuggets found their way into my mouth. Momma's sixth sense kicked in as she appeared at the kitchen door, "Now Kay, we won't have any for goodies if you keep that up."

I looked up at her, sighed a little, and then looked down at the seemingly endless pile of nuts — more determined than ever to get through it.

My task accomplished, I skipped across the kitchen to Momma's side and lifted up our treasure, meeting her smile with mine. We both knew what came next:

Butter Balls!

We filled the big metal mixing bowl with softened butter, sugar and flour. In went my freshly washed little hands to squish the ingredients together. Momma stood beside me, dropping handfuls of chopped pecans into the dough.

Then, we lined the cookie sheets on the countertop, rolled the dough into little balls, put them on the sheets and popped them in the oven. The sweet, buttery scent drifted all through the house.

When the cookies came out, we rolled them in powdered sugar, and I delivered them to Daddy and the boys who were in the living room pretending to be watching television. I knew they were really waiting for the cookies. With the first bite we knew that the Christmas season was here.

I've been away from my parents' home for more than 40 years, but for more than 30 years Momma sent me a big bag of already-shelled Missouri pecans for my Christmas treats.

This Christmas, baking Butter Balls will be one of my favorite ways to celebrate the season of love and good cheer.

Yes, it tugs at my heart that the pecans will come from Sam's Club instead of those great dancing trees out on the horizon. But still, I'll love making those powdered-sugared, pecan-laden delicacies to share with my family and friends. And as I eat more than my share, I will savor the memories of those Christmases long ago.

Butter Balls are more than mere family tradition; the truth is — it wouldn't be Christmas without them.

Butter Balls
A Harper Family Christmas Tradition

From the Missouri pecan groves to Christmas cookies. This story and recipe first appeared in a cookbook I wrote for my family to celebrate the cookies, cakes, and pies that had graced our table throughout my childhood. I hope you make them, and enjoy every bite!

Ingredients:

1 cup butter

5 tbsp sugar

3–31/2 cups flour

2 tsp vanilla

1 cup chopped pecans

Instructions:

Mix by hand. Roll into small balls. Line up on ungreased cookie sheets.

Bake at 350 degrees for 12 to 15 minutes.

Cool for a few minutes. Shake in a plastic bag filled with powdered sugar.

Prepare to eat and smile!

~ Kay Harper

36

Oh No! I've Lost Baby Jesus

It was Christmas. We had just moved into a new house and all the boxes were still packed, yet we had also invited guests for an open house the following week. A tape of "Sweet Little Jesus Boy" played in the background while I enjoyed the candles with their soft lights and fragrances of cinnamon and eggnog. They created just the right atmosphere to finish decorating and planning my menu.

I busily began decorating the dining table. I opened the box with the Christmas decorations, took out Mary and Joseph, and lovingly placed them in the center of the table. When I looked in the box for baby Jesus, he was not there!

I searched through the bubble wrap again. *He simply was not in that box.* I went back to the garage and frantically looked for boxes labeled Christmas… no baby Jesus!

Panic!

Now what? My heart froze. This just couldn't be happening. The deadline for the open house was fast approaching. It didn't help that my invited guests were several pastors and their wives from area churches. Not to have Jesus present with Mary and Joseph in the nativity was unthinkable!

I decided I'd just go buy a Baby Jesus, but no store would just sell the babe in the manger — and besides, the Nativity was a gift from our son and daughter-in-law. It was a beautiful collector set. Finding a babe to match was not a reality.

Time was fast-forwarding. Finally I decided to buy a rubber doll. I added a little bronzer to make it look ethnically appropriate, wrapped it in a flannel blanket, and hoped that no one would notice.

People were too gracious to comment on it at the open house; however, when the family came at Christmas, our three-year-old granddaughter did notice. She squealed with delight. "Grammy, is that my doll? Is it for me? Can I have it?" She took the little doll out of the manger, hugged him close, and added, "He's *kying* (crying) for me."

All through Christmas I kept thinking about losing Baby Jesus.

It consumed me.

Soon this will be a Christmas past, I told myself as I took a coffee break and sat staring at the Christmas tree. I watched the twinkling lights and thought about trying to buy a new baby Jesus.

But you really can't buy Jesus.

Then scriptures began flickering on and off in my mind. I remembered my husband's sermon about Simon the Sorcerer who wanted to buy Jesus' anointing. He thought it was magic. But it couldn't be bought.

The story of the rich young ruler flashed through my mind. He liked what he saw Jesus doing, and how he helped the people. He especially liked Jesus' personality. But he simply did not choose to make room for Jesus in his heart.

Then the precious scene of our little granddaughter kept replaying in my mind. I could hear her innocent words, "He's *kying* for me." I was reminded that he had sat outside Jerusalem and cried for his people. He loved them but they didn't recognize his deity.

After Christmas was over and all the decorations were packed away, I still looked for Baby Jesus. I kept thinking where I had seen him last. He had been displayed year 'round in our other house. We had a large yellow formal sunroom with an antique Queen Anne armoire that showcased a beautiful punch bowl collection and the collector nativity. I loved seeing Mary and Joseph with the Christ child on one of the shelves. I often would read my devotions and drink afternoon coffee in that room. It was so peaceful and wonderfully inspiring to be reminded of Jesus' birth, and celebrate his life by remembering the Bible stories that took place when he lived on earth. That's why I was so disappointed I had lost him.

One day after Christmas I opened a box of dishes, and — you guessed it — there was Baby Jesus in the manger. Not in the Christmas boxes but in a box of collectible glassware. No doubt, some friends who had helped pack the moving boxes had apparently thought he would be safer in the fragile glassware box.

Some people can't find Jesus. Others have found him and then put him in a box of their own choosing, of their own ideas. Many think about him just on Sunday while in church. Some intellectually cannot understand the simple truth that he isn't for sale. He gives himself to us simply because he loves us. Some people don't feel like they need him.

This caused me to think about a particular blind man I know who had found Jesus as his Savior. One day the man told me, "I had to go blind to see."

Some have convinced themselves they aren't good enough to invite Jesus into their homes or hearts. And some people think he doesn't exist.

My heart felt so happy and peaceful to once again have Mary, Joseph and the Christmas Child together. Just in time to begin the New Year.

I lovingly placed the Baby Jesus with the rest of the nativity, grateful for the lesson He had taught me in seeking his presence.

~ Barbara Wells

37

Making Unforgettable Memories

My husband and I moved from Pennsylvania to South Carolina in 2001. We brought my mother with us. A lot happened in those years from 2001 to 2015. We built a lovely home on Lake Greenwood, and hosted much of our family and northern friends for visits, ranging from overnight to several weeks.

For as long as I can remember, the Christmas holiday was the highlight of my year. It started with decorating our home, then the tree, and helping decorate the church. Interests moved on to purchasing and wrapping special gifts, the filling of stockings, and the smell of pine and cinnamon that permeated every room of our home. But nothing could surpass greeting each other with hugs, all the great conversations and raucous laughter, and the quiet moments of praising God who sent his son to offer us salvation.

Christmas is a time of wonderful family memories.

In 2007 my mother, who had lived with us for 12 years, moved into a nursing facility. In October of that same year, my husband moved on to the church triumphant. My dog, who I had only rescued a few months earlier, and I, decided not to decorate a house that no one saw but us. Except for Christmas activities offered at our church, it was the unfortunate beginning of Bah-Humbug Christmases for us.

Sometimes I was offended that my friends didn't think of me when they were having so much fun with their families. I began to even dislike Facebook because of all the photos of families together, making special memories.

The approach of Thanksgiving and Christmas was a dismal concern. Envy had never before been a part of my life. I chastised myself as I read over-and-over, Chapter 13 of 1 Corinthians, about love not being envious.

I appreciated why my northern family didn't ask me to join them. It was, after all, winter with lots of snow, and ice, and cold. I'm sure I probably had said, at one-time-or-another, that driving a car alone, for 14 hours through the mountains, during winter, was not for me.

For six years I endured not-so-special, very lonely, Christmases. I determined 2015 was the year for a different approach. I perused the Internet and found fairly good deals for air travel and rental cars. I was committed to the trek to the frozen tundra of northwestern Pennsylvania. It would be my first Christmas north in over 15 years. I was going to spend it with my sister and her family, to be followed by a few days with a friend, and a celebration of the New Year with my stepdaughter and her family.

In the weeks prior to leaving, when Thanksgiving weather generated thousands of cancelled flights and stranded travelers, I questioned the sanity of making the trip. The day finally arrived. After standing in the airport screening line for x-rays and pat-downs, I was soon flying through the air, just like Santa.

My first delight of the season was my seatmate, who turned out to be a delightful young person. We enjoyed learning about each other, keeping up a constant stream of give-and-take conversation throughout the entire flight, even exchanging business cards before disembarking.

The days with my sister, niece, nephew and family were more than just special. It brought with it a new acceptance of the craziness of life and of individual idiosyncrasies, which is very important when your quiet life suddenly is filled with rooms of people, all talking, laughing, clapping and jumping up-and-down.

Christmas Eve dinner was followed by a service at a large sandstone church where the outdoor nativity set was absent the baby Jesus, who traditionally would not be placed in the manger until after his birth, on Christmas morning.

Two lit trees, filled with decorations depicting scenes of the blessed birth of Christ, adorned the front of the church. Candles flaming brightly in glass chimneys graced the end of each pew down the center aisle. The choir sang like angels from heaven.

With perfect timing, teams began to extinguish every light in the church until, in total blackness, the preacher unfolded the story of Creation. Dramatically, in the silence of darkness, Old Testament highlights were retold, with candles lit as God's promises were revealed. With the telling of the birth of the baby Jesus, the Christ candle was lit, giving hope to the world.

The story continued with the star, the angels, the shepherds and the wise men. Advent candles, pew candles and tree lights shone. The melodious tones of *Silent Night* filled the sanctuary.

As everyone made their way into the dark night following the closing prayer, people stopped and, murmuring, pointed upward. A ring, like the ring around Saturn, encircled the moon. I believe it was a sign, a memory I will never forget, that Christ was giving us his assurance, on this Christmas Eve, he was still lighting our way.

The next day was filled with the gift exchange, good food, great fellowship and family fun.

During that trip north I spent the days between Christmas and New Year's Eve with a special friend and then ended the old year and began the new one with my stepdaughter, her husband, and their two sons, wives and children.

New Year's Eve with four children under the age of four, two rambunctious boys and two sweet little girls, would bring mountains of joy to even the most dried up heart.

At 8 p.m. the celebration began. Baby Jenna was content in her daddy's arms while Lukas, Andrew, and Lauren provided entertainment and laughter.

They squealed with delight while watching The Little Mermaid, Mr. Peabody and Sherman, and Elsa, from *Frozen* doing their version of the ten-to-one final New Year's countdown.

With each count down, the children, hats on and horns blowing, marched around the great room. Peals of laughter filled the house as they kicked at the large inflated balloons their dads dropped from the upstairs balcony.

For me, this family event topped what tens of thousands observe each New Year's Eve as the crystal ball is dropped in New York City's Times Square.

By midnight I was in bed, thinking about the happiest holiday I'd had in years.

One should not be alone for the holidays if there is any other way. Family is to be enjoyed and savored, while making unforgettable memories.

Already, I'm looking forward to next Christmas!

~ Toni Armstrong Sample

The Bread Returned

A familiar quote from Ecclesiastes 11:1 NIV states: Cast your bread upon the waters, for after many days you will find it again. Some people understand this verse to mean that when we give to help others, in the future in some way, help will be given to us. This happened to a member of my family.

For several years at Christmas time when my children were young, we had fun giving gifts anonymously. We lived in a small town of 400 people; it was usually common knowledge when anyone needed help. We bought gifts not only for children, but also for adults. They weren't expensive gifts, but were chosen with each individual in mind.

One year my younger daughter, Cathy, wanted to give gifts to a classmate and her family because their finances were limited. The gifts were placed on the family's porch and we sat in our car at a distance, watching to see that the gifts were taken into the house.

Years passed, my children had become adults and married. Cathy's husband, after having had four strokes and a heart transplant, eventually became an invalid and was confined to a hospital bed at home. Cathy carried a heavy load as she worked and then went home to care for her husband.

Most of her salary was used to pay for sitters for her husband while she was gone. Cathy had to work, not only for financial reasons but also because they needed her insurance to pay the many medical expenses.

That year at Christmas time, an anonymous person left a well-filled box of gifts on Cathy's porch. As she opened the gifts in the box, she thought about those times, when as a young girl she had taken part in leaving gifts on other people's porches.

Now she had received gifts in the same way. She had cast bread in her childhood; when she was an adult the bread had returned. The promise of Ecclesiastes 11:1 was fulfilled.

~ Norma C. Mezoe

Are You Broken This Christmas?

M oney was tight that first Christmas. So tight that when we bought an artificial tree for $30 and it went on sale the following week, we stuffed it back in the box and returned it.

By the time we'd made our way to the garden center, the sales clerk had hauled back the tree we'd just returned, and we bought it again for ten dollars less. We bought three bags of red and white satin ornaments with the refund.

Unfortunately, even though the tree wasn't very big, the bags of cheap balls didn't go very far.

The next day we were grocery shopping when a bin of ornaments caught my eye. The sign read Four for One Dollar, which sounded too good to be true. As I examined each bagged wooden ornament, I saw why they were so cheap — they were all broken. A little girl on skis lacked a pole, a mouse dressed to look like a Wise Man was missing the red ball on his nose, and a bear on a rocking horse needed a wheel.

"They're all broken," I said, dismissing them and moving on.

My husband looked closer. "All the parts are here. I think I can fix them."

"That's too much work. They're not worth it."

"I'd like to try," he said. "I think I love them."

And fix them he did. With painstaking care and incredible patience, he glued each broken part, even creatively improvising when the pieces were too damaged to be restored. When the glue dried, he hung the ornaments on the tree among the satin balls.

"See," he said with a smile, "I told you I could fix them."

Since that first Christmas, we've added many ornaments to our tree. We replaced the satin balls long ago, but every year we continue to hang the little wooden ornaments. They remind us of how far we've come, how blessed we are, and what God did for us on the very first Christmas.

Like the ornaments in the bin, we were practically worthless. Broken and discarded, we weren't much to look at, but God took pity on us.

"I think I can fix them," God said. "I'd like to try. I love them."

And with painstaking care and incredible patience, he applied the blood of Jesus to every broken part, even creatively improvising when parts of us were too damaged to be restored. And then he added us to his family tree and smiled.

"See," he said, "I told you I could fix them."

What's your story this Christmas?

It's as if God is saying: "I want to repair your broken parts and place you in my family tree. I want you to know Jesus, your Savior."

Do you know him as your Savior? If you do, rejoice. If you don't, don't wait another day to accept his gift of healing and wholeness.

You've lived broken long enough. It's time to let God make you whole.

~ Lori Hatcher

40

Christmas in July

After a battery of tests and extensive interviews I was hired by the elders and pastor of Crossroads Fellowship of Raleigh, North Carolina to be their second pastoral staff member and their first-ever youth pastor. At that time we had more than 300 people attending our worship services, which were held in the auditorium of a local high school.

Being new, I wanted to start off with a bang so I wrote to some of the most respected youth pastors in the country. I asked them if they were to launch a new ministry in a city with a church which had the potential to eventually turn into a mega-church, what they would suggest.

To my surprise I received over 60 responses out of 100 requests. Many offered good advice, which I applied as time went on. Probably the best advice I received was from Rick Caldwell of Little Rock, Arkansas. Rick was the college roommate of former Arkansas Governor Mike Huckabee. For over 15 years he has helped men around the world in his discipleship series, *Authentic Manhood*, to experience the life of truth, passion, and purpose they were created to live.

Rick has a diverse background that includes traveling nationally as a conference speaker, running a family land development business, and serving as a senior advisor on a Presidential campaign. In 1999, he served as the founding director of ShareFest, a strategic, bridge-building event that united over 100 central Arkansas churches and 8,000 volunteers in an effort to demonstrate God's love to the community.

Rick's advice was basic but insightful. He suggested, "Kick off your ministry with a big event and make sure it is dynamic — something people will remember and talk about for weeks."

That was great advice which I intended to follow, but I had a few concerns. We had no church building and only 20 to 30 students in grades 6 through 12. We had a fair budget considering the size of our student ministry, but not enough money to pull off a humongous initial event for students. I did not think the budget committee would be impressed if I spent my yearly budget on my first event.

I did what I usually do when nothing else is working. I prayed and prayed and prayed and prayed. Someone suggested that we might help children who were having difficulties. I thought that a great idea, so I asked around. Invariably the name mentioned was the Baptist Children's Home.

I called the director of the children's home and shared my desire to minister to the children and his staff. He was polite and grateful for my offer but his answer was not what I expected. He shared that countless churches annually contact him with a desire to minister to the children during Thanksgiving or during the Christmas holiday. He said, "If you could come any another time of the year we'd welcome you with opens arms."

Just then, as quick as clicking your fingers, God gave me an idea. I asked, "Would you be open to us throwing a Christmas-in-July celebration on the 25th of July?

He said, "You're on!"

What occurred was beyond our wildest dreams and expectations. A huge number of students and parents participated. They brought gifts galore, including bicycles, sports equipment, dolls, clothes, and gift certificates for movies, sporting events, hair salons and skating rinks.

The Christmas meal we prepared was one of the largest non-restaurant buffets I have ever seen. There was steak, turkey, ham, roast beef, chicken and everything else imaginable ranging from hamburgers and hotdogs, to pizza and corn dogs. There were numerous side dishes, beverages and more desserts than most All-You-Can-Eat buffets would even dream of serving.

After dinner we sang Christmas carols, decorated the Christmas tree, and I read the Christmas story from the Bible. Many children and adults prayed and made commitments to follow Jesus. We then proceeded to open presents. Wow! The joy on their faces was a memory I, and others, will never forget.

The evening had been so incredible our students and chaperones didn't want to leave. Many of the children pleaded to stay longer. Our visit was approaching six hours. We stated for the umpteenth time that we had to leave because their parents would become concerned about their safety and whereabouts.

I also found it hard to leave, but I also was well aware that we still had a 90-minute drive ahead of us. After getting into our van, we all agreed that our Christmas in July celebration was one of their best Christmases ever!

As we drove away I asked those in my 15-passenger van, "What made tonight so special?"

The students all began talking at once. It seemed everyone couldn't stop talking about the events. One said, "I don't think I ever experienced so much joy and happiness."

"Yeah," a student agreed, "There was no drama tonight. It seemed like everyone was more focused on making others happy rather than themselves.

Another commented, "None of the children from the children's home acted selfish. It seemed they were generally happy for those who got presents as much as receiving their own."

One boy said, "That never happens at my house."

A quiet young man who rarely spoke out said, "I have never felt so much love in one room."

Another commented, "Yeah, I never have gotten so many hugs in my entire life as I did tonight." He paused a long time, then repeated, "Ever...in my life."

Another student shared, "Wouldn't it be great if we celebrated Christmas several times a year as a reminder to love God and love others?"

The long ride through a dark countryside brought a blanket of fatigue covering the majority of students and adults in the van. During that prolonged silence (everyone else was asleep except the driver — me) as I drove on the deserted rural road a thought occurred to me. *They will know we are Christians by our love.* I thought of the ways our students demonstrated love for the orphaned children. Then how we were loved by children who had more "have-nots" than "haves."

Thanks God, it truly was an unbelievable night! *Christmas in July.* I chuckled softly to myself. Who would have ever thought having Christmas in July would turn into a life-changing event for so many!

~ *Tommy Scott Gilmore, III*

41

Something About Mary

Many times in life, the significance of a certain moment does not become fully apparent until years down the road. Perhaps it is because of the inevitable sources of distraction that exist in each moment, or maybe our feeble brains are not great at grasping the bigger picture of an occurrence which doesn't stand out as life-altering. Regardless, there is something about time and experience that highlights the value of past events.

Hindsight unveils significance.

I didn't spend a lot of time in church as a young child. I understood that Christmas was about a baby who was born many years ago, but as many children do, I set my eyes on what I could get out of the holiday. In my early teenage years, my mom starting taking my sister and me to church regularly. We quickly became active members. Many of the young girls were part of an interpretive movement group that performed during the church service on special occasions. I wasn't particularly interested in being in front of a large crowd of intimidating adults, but participation was a great reason to spend more hours with friends.

Our interpretive movement group always played a part in the Christmas Eve service. One year, we prepared a beautiful interpretation that went along with the song "Mary, Did You Know?" Although I did not love being in the spotlight, I found myself slightly envious of the girl who got to walk down the aisle as Mary. It was a little strange to see this 13-year-old walking awkwardly toward the altar carrying a swaddled baby doll, but I wanted to be her. Even with limited knowledge of the Christmas story, I knew enough to know that Mary was special. She was called by God to do an important task. She had every reason to be admired for her humble obedience. Something about her role was attractive.

I wondered what it would be like to have a baby. I wondered what it would be like to feel close to God. I wondered what a young girl had to do to earn his favor like Mary did.

That night became more than a performance for me. It stirred up questions I had never considered.

I didn't think about that particular night very often over the next few years. In fact, it wasn't until about 12 years later that I gave it much thought. In December 2011, I was pregnant with my first son. "Mary, Did You Know?" came on my car radio, and I could hardly contain my emotion. Call it hormones, fatigue, or maturity; regardless, I heard the song through a different perspective. I was overcome with gratitude and love for the Creator of life who was entrusting me with another life. I was overcome with gratitude for his love for me, which was so great that he sent that sweet innocent baby to save my soul.

I was overcome with gratitude for Mary, that teenage girl who humbly accepted her calling. I felt a connection with her that I had not felt as a teenager. I wondered if she had been scared to deliver a baby. I wondered if she had been excited about becoming a mother or if she was more confused by the whole event. I wondered if she grasped the magnitude of her role.

Each Christmas, I go back to the night when I first began pondering the birth of my Savior. I am grateful for my mom who took me to church. I am grateful for the church family who helped guide me into a life of faith. Ultimately, I am grateful for the God who is constantly reaching out to us, regardless of our age, maturity, or influence.

~ Kristin Dossett

42

The Good Samaritan's Christmas Gift

I stood by the kitchen sink with a pile of Christmas cards to seal. Christmas 2013 would arrive in a few days, and I hoped the cards would be received on time. While catching drips of water for sealing, I startled at the unexpected sound of a yowling cat. After our two outdoor cats had passed away some years back, I had continued putting out food scraps for any wanderers. The sounds were like cats in a dispute. I thought I'd better go help sort it out.

I walked around the corner of the house, and at first didn't see the yowling one. Then looking closer, I saw it on the front porch, and I did a double take at its appearance. Expecting to see a large cat, I thought to myself, *what in the world is that thing?* A tiny black and white kitten stared at me, and it had some ugly marking on its face. That was the ugliest kitten I had ever seen. It looked like Hitler. It had a black and white face with a black mustache on the white by its nose and mouth.

My husband, Art, had been getting his shower before work. I waited outside the bathroom door with the strange kitten in my arms. He opened the door.

"Look what I found on our porch," I said and smiled.

Art reached out to pet the little lost kitten. "Do you have any idea how it got there?"

"I think it must be a neighbor's escapee Christmas gift," I said. "I'll call around and see."

"That seems likely. It looks odd with the mustache. You know, it almost seems like someone drew on it with a black marker as a mean joke."

We were empty nesters, and did not want the cost of upkeep, and the trouble of finding care for an animal while traveling. Our next trip, scheduled right after Christmas, did not include plans for a pet carrier. Art finished getting ready for work and soon left. I took the kitten back outside and tried to feed it a little tuna, the only food I had it might like. Poor thing! Rooting around in my hand, it seemed like it wanted to nurse rather than eat food.

I called the neighbors, assuming someone would be happy I found their lost kitten.

"No, we have a dog. I'd like to help, but we can't take in a kitten. You could take it to the Humane Society," suggested the neighbor.

"No, we don't know anyone around here who has lost a kitten," said another neighbor.

"Well," I said, "Please let me know if you hear of anyone who would like a kitten. We can't keep it. Vacation's next week."

Then I called my friend who loves cats. Surely she and her husband would want a kitten since their two cats appeared near the end of their lives. Maybe they could keep the kitten during our trip.

I sent them a picture of the kitten by email. It looked rather cute in the photo, and would clean up nicely. At first they expressed the thought that although an odd looking creature, its uniqueness generated a special appeal. They showed their daughter the picture. She told them about an Internet website devoted to Kitlers, cats which look like Hitler. Their interest in the kitten brought forth a promise to think about giving it a home.

Progress! My family had to leave in a few days for our trip. I decided to take the kitten by their home and hold it in the car so they could at least see it in person. They adored it.

"Zappa," said my friend's husband, "it looks like Zappa." Already considering names! Good sign, however, they still needed to think seriously about taking the kitten because of the older cats. I could tell they were torn.

"I'm sorry," apologized my friend later on the phone, "we decided we can't take in a stray kitten that might bring disease to Cupcake and Nala."

I could tell her heart tugged between having the joy of a kitten and the duty of caring for her older cats. Her husband really wanted the kitten, too. I did not want them to feel guilty over their decision. I accepted what must happen. I admitted I had started to bond with the tiny kitten with the big purrs and squeaky meow.

I made another call. "Dekalb Animal Hospital," said a cheerful voice on the phone.

"A kitten showed up at our house, and we are leaving for vacation soon. How much does it cost to board a kitten for a week?"

"It's twenty dollars a night, but the kitten will need to first be seen by the vet, get its shots, and be treated for fleas."

"Ouch! I see. Well, I guess I need to bring him in."

"Let me check the vet's appointment book. When do you need boarding?"

We got everything set up for our new kitten, Bosley, to board. I did not know where his name came from except maybe God gave it to me. Bosley means, "meadow near the woods," coincidentally similar to our son's name, Wesley, which means, "western meadow."

During the appointment with the vet, a special comb raked through Bosley's fur and revealed fleas. As the vet went through the various routine checks, I heard her say, "Bosley is a girl." With the mustache, Bosley had looked like a boy. We simply added the appropriate title to revise her name to Miss Bosley.

I hated leaving her, but felt I had no choice. I knew she would be in good care. The staff adored the tiny kitten with the mustache. They promised to take her out of the cage and pet her so she would not be afraid of people. I found it hard to believe we owned a kitten, or rather, a Kitler, just in time for Christmas and vacation.

Miss Bosley has been with us for over two years. She has filled our empty nest with joy, laughter, and at times panic as she has tested limits and performed crazy kitten stunts. We discovered she likes to retrieve paper balls that we throw to her, and she tries to catch them midair, so she has qualities of a dog. She loves to cuddle and sit in laps and purr. She can be aggravating when trying to get our attention by scratching on the television screen or the computer monitor. Lately I have found a shrill whistle will make her stop. Since she is the color of a border collie, I prefer to think of her as a border cat rather than as a Kitler. She has grown into a beautiful cat.

Thinking back on how Miss Bosley showed up on our porch at one of the worst possible times, and how I could not find any other place for her to stay, made me remember the story in the Bible of the Good Samaritan who provided for the man he could have passed by.

He paid for his lodging and care.

I took on the role of Good Samaritan to Miss Bosley. Through my kindness to her, I found that God returned the favor with blessings worth far more than I had paid for her boarding and care. I received a good and perfect gift from God which far exceeded anything I could have imagined or realized I needed. Miss Bosley, the Good Samaritan's Christmas gift, keeps on purring year after year.

~ *Janice S. Garey*

43

Do You Believe?

Do you still believe in Santa Claus?" I casually asked my nine-year-old while driving a few weeks ago. He looked at me with big puppy dog eyes. The kind with a hint of sadness and uncertainty that can melt a mama's heart in two seconds.

His first response was, "Mom, I don't want you to be mad."

"Why would I be mad?" I asked him.

He said he knew Santa wasn't real because he'd looked through the key hole of his door last Christmas and saw me putting gifts under the tree.

I realized that moment last year was as if reality slapped him in the face. All he knew of Christmas, up to that point, was decorating Christmas trees, presents with shiny bows and the story of Jesus' birth somewhere in the middle. But the exciting anticipation was about Santa. I'm sure he wondered what else I wasn't truthful about. I imagined he said to himself: "If Santa isn't real then what else isn't?"

Later, after researching some facts on St. Nick, I sat down with him to share the knowledge and open up conversation.

"No, the Santa you know is not real. He doesn't live at the North Pole with elves who make toys. However, St. Nicholas was a real man."

I talked to him about the facts I held in my hand on a piece of paper. Nicholas was born in the third century in modern day Turkey. He was raised as a devout Christian. The words Jesus spoke to the rich young ruler about selling what he had and give to the poor, also spoke to Nicholas, and he obeyed.

Nicholas used his inheritance to assist the needy, the sick, and the suffering. He dedicated his life to serving God and was made Bishop of Myra while still young. Bishop Nicholas became known throughout the land for his generosity to those in need, his love for children, and his concern for sailors and ships.

After his death on December 6, elaborate feasts were held each year on that date and small gifts were given to children, usually in their shoes, in his honor.

The Dutch began a tradition of Sinterklaas that turned into Santa Claus in America. From there, St. Nicholas was morphed into a plump, jolly man in a red suit, in his magic sleigh, who delivers gifts to children of the world.

"But, at Christmas, we're not celebrating Santa or Nicholas. We celebrate the most wonderful time of year because our Savior was born," I told him. "We give gifts because God gave us the gift of Jesus."

Many questions followed as he came to better understand the true meaning of Christmas. While he knows the reason for the season, I want him to use the imagination God has given him. To keep the wonder and enchantment in his heart.

I understand the exciting traditions of cookies for Santa. Listening for reindeer on the roof. Presents under the tree. I still enjoy all of these at the age of 36. However, this Christmas and all that may follow, we will make Happy Birthday Jesus cookies.

Before waiting for magical reindeer and wrapped packages, we will pause and be still as the Holy Spirit wraps us in his presence. The joy, hope and peace that we want to experience at Christmas can be with us year 'round. And it all started when a virgin conceived and bore a son whose name is Jesus.

– Dianna Owens

A Cockeyed Christmas

As a struggling quasi perfectionist, it bugged me that our nativity scene figures had been messed up. In fact, you could see only their backs. It was the Christmas season of 2001 that our three-year-old daughter, Maddie, with limited supervision from her dad, set up the manger scene. I was close by, busily unpacking holiday ornaments and breakables. Scurrying about, I tried to find the perfect out-of-reach spot to position a delicate angel or fragile Santa. I fussed with bows. I primped with garland. You get the picture.

A few days later, I slowed for a rare slice of quiet in my day. As a mother of two children under the age of three, I savored an ordered, peaceful house. With Maddie at school and her baby brother, Owen, tucked tightly in his crib upstairs, I ate my lunch in blessed silence. But when I glanced up to the china hutch in our breakfast room, I noticed something was amiss in Bethlehem.

Like three linebackers, the wise men were huddled close together, their backs to me, blocking the other key players. I got up to peer closer and caught a glimpse of Mary, tightly ensconced next to Joseph. There was little breathing room for a curious donkey. It was only after craning my neck to peer around one of the wise men that I could finally manage a peek at baby Jesus in his manger. The Christ child was completely blocked from view by his parents and visitors from the East.

My first reaction was to fix the assembly, spacing each figure symmetrically until I was satisfied with the scene's aesthetic appeal. I reached to adjust a wise man but at once I was struck, and then humbled, by my daughter's deliberate, careful placement of the grouping.

Maybe Maddie knew a sacred secret. Perhaps, through the lens of child-like faith, she shared the same excitement and anticipation as those who sought the Christ child 2,000 years ago. Her decorating efforts reminded me to do as the words of a song recommends, "Come adore on bended knee, Christ the Lord, the newborn King." Perhaps I should draw in close to the baby, as an eager three-year-old might do.

That day, I made a pact with myself. A pact to simplify, to cut out the unnecessary and savor the purest joys of the season. As parents of preschoolers, my husband and I were blessed to have constant reminders of the sacred. We relished the simple joys of the season through their awestruck eyes.

A few days after my daughter's decorating lesson, I visited my friend Cathy's home. After taking off my coat, I turned around to behold their Christmas tree. It was…interesting…to say the least. In her quest to embrace the child-like wonder of the season, Cathy proudly explained that her tree designers were Sarah, age four and Andrew, age two.

Her two children did it "all by themselves" while she was cooking dinner in the kitchen. Not only did the ornaments adorn only the lower third of the tree, but their great enthusiasm kept them from waiting for the box of ornaments Cathy had yet to pull down from the attic. Instead, the children improvised, adorning the spruce limbs with stuffed animals and other colorful toys.

"They were so proud when they finished." She smiled proudly. "I couldn't bear to touch it!"

That Christmas, I followed my friend's lead and took notes from my daughter. I allowed the beautiful imperfections to show. The tree had lopsided, glue and glitter laden, Styrofoam bells instead of color-coordinated, store bought bows and balls. Several gifts were wrapped with *lots* of tape and mismatched ribbons. The angel cookies looked a little like Michelin tire men with *extra* sprinkles. The words to "Rudolph" had a different ring to them. And if you paused long enough and looked carefully enough, you couldn't miss it: the joy behind every cockeyed ornament and off-key Christmas carol.

May your days be merry and bright and may all your Christmases be a little off center.

~ Maresa DePuy

45

Christmas Day Miracle

My dad was a plumber by trade and had his own heating and plumbing business. It was physically demanding at times, but Dad repeatedly told us how he liked to help people. He felt it was his calling.

One day in the early summer of 1968, while carrying a bathtub to a second floor bathroom, he injured his back and excruciating pain confined him to bed. After several doctors' appointments, there was still no definitive diagnosis. MRIs and CT scans did not exist. One doctor diagnosed arthritis; another suggested back traction. My dad was really suffering and was willing to try anything. He wanted and needed to get better. He was not able to work. No work meant no money, and he had a family to support.

Each evening our angels of mercy, Uncle Moe and Uncle Ed, came over to help my dad get out of bed and walk from the bedroom to the bathroom. It was like a baby taking the first steps. I worried my dad would never get better. I worried he would never walk again by himself. How would my mom handle three children, ages four, seven, and 12, and a bedridden husband?

However, in this time of trial, the Lord gave her extraordinary grace of strength and perseverance. Mom was a remarkable woman who handled it all with no complaint.

I recall Mom whispering to her sister Gerry on the telephone, "The doctors have to do something. Jack can't go on like this. We need a miracle." Maybe my young ears were not supposed to hear that, but it went from my lips straight to the ears of Jesus. I knew he would listen.

As I think back to that time, over 40 years ago, the words of my mother echo in my mind. "I'm praying that your father gets well. If the good Lord makes him better, I will never ask for anything for myself in life." My mother was faithful to this promise throughout her life. When she passed away in 2010, I'm certain the good Lord rewarded her abundantly for her faithfulness.

Day after day, she assured Dad he would get better, walk again, and be able to go back to work. "Just have faith and pray," she repeated again and again.

A span of three months may not seem like much time, but to a child, this time of sickness seemed like forever. Dad remained confined to bed and unable to walk on his own. He became depressed. It was 1968 and the technological advances for medical diagnosis were very limited.

I thought our miracle came in October 1968 when they finally diagnosed my dad with a herniated lumbar disc and he underwent surgery. The doctors said the surgery was successful, but Dad still could not walk without assistance. There seemed to be no answer to this problem. Dad gave up any hope of getting well. He thought he would never walk again.

Our family's faith was strong. We believed the Lord heard our prayers and would answer our plea for help in time. Christmas morning 1968, my dad followed his morning routine. I don't know how it began, but before my eyes, Dad walked from the bedroom, one small step at a time, toward the living room where the Christmas tree stood, shiny with tinsel and colored lights.

"Daddy's walking! Daddy's walking!" I hollered, standing with my younger sister in the hallway by our living room on Christmas morning. Tears ran down our cheeks as we repeated, "Daddy's walking! Daddy's walking!" Our piercing screams penetrated the early morning quiet. Mother ran from the kitchen to see what was happening.

"Look, Mom, look! Daddy's walking! Santa Claus came and gave us the best Christmas present we ever got," I said.

"Santa didn't give us this present," Mom said. "Jesus did. He heard our prayers and he answered just like I told you he would. The good Lord has given us a Christmas miracle. That's why your Dad is walking."

It was our best Christmas ever. We had presents under the Christmas tree, but the best present was the miracle Jesus brought. Dad was able to walk without help. It was a gift our family never forgot.

It was our Christmas Day Miracle!

~ Beverly Sce

46

Be an Eliza

Eliza, our four-year-old granddaughter, was eager to go to the Christmas Eve service at the local church that sponsored her preschool. We were eager to take her. The pastor called the children up to sit with her during the children's sermon. Next to her was an empty crèche. She invited the children to search for and bring back the missing figures she had previously hidden in plain view throughout the church.

The kids, Eliza among them, were on the job immediately, raucously running around looking for sheep and angels and magi. She ran to me, with excitement in her voice and showed me the figurine she had found. "Look, Mimi, I found Jesus!"

God desires us to experience the same enthusiasm and joy as Eliza in the finding of the Messiah, the saving one. In the same way that pastor left obvious clues for the children to find, God leaves us clues throughout creation and in our hearts in an attempt to awake our curiosity enough to seek the Messiah.

When God wanted to get Moses' attention, he lit a bush on fire. Moses was minding his own business, tending his flock, but said, "Amazing! Why isn't that bush burning up? I must go over and see this" (Exodus 3:3). Moses' curiosity led him to the place where he encountered God.

At a time when Judah was in need of rescue from an opposing army, the prophet Isaiah told King Ahaz God planned to deliver him. He told him to "ask a sign of the Lord your God." Ahaz thought this was uncool and not very spiritual. He said, "I will not ask, I will not put the Lord to the test." "Alright then," responded God, "since you are afraid to ask for a sign, I myself will give you a sign. 'Look, the young woman is with child and shall bear a son, and shall name him Emmanuel.'"

God leaves clues, hoping to get our attention. The greatest clue is Christmas. The origin of the word itself is a combination of the words *Christ's Mass*. Today some have renamed Christmas the Holiday Season, perhaps unaware the word *holiday* also has a Christian origin: the Old English words for Holy Day.

Our homes, our streets, our stores are brightly decorated. Christmas lights abound, reminding us that light breaks into darkness, and in fact, light triumphs over darkness. Let's celebrate! Christmas declares: Love invades the world.

All the activities that accompany this season are clues. Shopping for the perfect gift that will bring joy and pleasure to our loved one tells the story of God's heart of love toward us. God wants us to have perfect joy and complete pleasure. The happiness of gathering with friends and co-workers is a shadow of the happiness God wants to share with his friends. Preparation for Christmas dinner reminds us of the great feast awaiting us in heaven, one that will satisfy all our longings.

The holiday season is a busy time of year, lots of shopping to do, parties to attend, meals to plan. I'm not going to suggest that we slow down and remember the meaning of the season. Instead, I want to be a Moses — tending my flock and looking for burning bushes!

Each of us should be like Eliza and look for signs of the Messiah hidden in plain sight.

~ Debby Bellingham

47

My Watching Angel

The room is dark except for the Christmas tree lights. The brightest is the angel at the top. As I snuggle in my cozy lounge chair with a cup of hot chocolate, the aroma brings back memories of the first time I saw the angel on that special Christmas so long ago.

December 1950. She was sitting next to a lovely glass ornament on a gift-shop shelf in Anchorage, Alaska. We debated the merits of each for some time.

"We have to decide," I told my husband. "We can't afford both."

He chuckled. "Not on the salary the Air Force pays corporals."

"The glass ornament is tall and elegant," I said, "and the design on it is beautiful."

"But it doesn't have long blonde hair like the angel," Clair teased as he looked down at me. "And I really like long blonde hair."

The choice was made. The angel with the golden hair would sit at the top of our first Christmas tree. Clair caught the attention of a nearby sales clerk.

The clerk put the angel on the counter, expressing surprise that it was on that particular shelf. "There's a better selection of angels at the end of this aisle," he said. "Apparently this one was misplaced."

Assured we were satisfied, he placed the angel in a box. We gathered our purchases and hurried out into the sub-zero cold. The warmth of our house would be a welcomed refuge.

"I'm ready to begin decorating," Clair said. The fir tree was already set up in the corner of the living room. He removed the decorations from their wrappings while I made hot chocolate. Between sips, we hung lights, ornaments and tinsel.

"This will be the crowning touch," Clair said as he placed the angel on the top branch.

We stood close together to admire our handiwork. The glowing angel was the perfect contrast to the blue tree lights shimmering against the ornaments and silver tinsel.

Clair smiled. "She's beautiful, just like the other blonde in my life."

"Except this blonde is not carrying a wand and does not wear a silver skirt covered with glittering stars," I replied.

He laughed. "The halo also seems to be missing."

I leaned my head on his shoulder as he put his arm around me. For a brief moment I pictured the tall glass ornament in the place of the angel. It might be a valuable collector's item some day. The thought passed quickly. Clair was right. Although the delicate ornament was beautiful, it would never be more than an ornament. The angel was different. She had personality. She would watch over us and the family we planned to have.

For nine more Christmases the angel's watch would include only Clair and me — until Laura was born in July 1960, and Nancy in June 1962. The angel seemed to glow brighter after they came. Perhaps it was because her light now reflected in the eyes of two little girls filled with wonder at the sight of a Christmas angel with long golden hair.

Each holiday season my angel watched from her perch at the top of trees selected after our daughters declared them to be the very best on the tree farm. Not only was my angel beautiful, she was incredibly brave. There were times when keeping her watch meant clinging perilously to the top of a tree cut from the side of a hill.

She kept watch and smiled late into pre-Christmas evenings while I secretly sewed doll clothes and Clair patiently struggled with those "easy to assemble" toys. On Christmas mornings, she lit the way as two pajama-clad little girls rushed downstairs to find their gifts from Santa.

So many memories — my first Christmas with Clair, the magic of Christmas reflected in the eyes of small children, the deep sadness of my first Christmas without my husband. My angel watches with me as the memories drift by, just as she has done for over 60 years.

From her vantage point, she has watched her reflection in glass ornaments as old as she is. They display colorful frosted designs and tiny inset winter scenes. All, like me, have faded a little with age. All, like my 59-year marriage, are a treasure.

As each year passed, my angel watched new ornaments join the old. A miniature tractor because Clair loved farms. A tiny motor home reminiscent of travels and campfires. An ornament from Austria that plays "Silent Night" bought on our fiftieth-anniversary trip. A hand-carved Santa from a friend. An exquisite Art Deco ornament from Laura. A papier-mâché face Nancy made in first grade. The face is an atrocious shade of green, with equally dreadful colors of purple, yellow and burgundy poked by young fingers to form eyes, nose and mouth. No wonder my angel is smiling.

This evening as I end the watch with my angel, I recall again that first Christmas when Clair and I were newlyweds. We were far from family and far from God. We lingered such a long time deciding between the delicate glass ornament and the plastic angel with long golden hair. It was the lighted angel we could not resist.

I am convinced it was God who nudged us in her direction. Contrary to the clerk's assumption, the plastic angel had not been misplaced. She was exactly where she was supposed to be. God knew what we needed before we did. He knew that a Christmas was coming when I would have far more need for the plastic angel than for an exquisite antique glass ornament. "I know the plans I have for you," declares the LORD, "plans to prosper you and not to harm you, plans to give you hope and a future" (Jeremiah 29:11 NIV).

With only a few days remaining in the holiday season, I will soon tuck away my watching angel for another year. I will miss her shining presence. She has brightened my Christmas and dulled the ache of loneliness. Her light has brought me comfort and helped to diminish the shadow of grief that descended upon me after my husband's death.

She reminds me that memories eventually do create more joy than sorrow.

~ *Carolyn Roth Barnum*

✦ 48 ✦

Fearfully and Wonderfully Made

T he laughter and joy within the Sunday school classroom electrified me. From 2 years old to 12, all the children were high on the love of Jesus. A high that would be hard to duplicate.

Sunday school teachers anchored little angel wings to the white costumes. The students' worship leader offered his "C" note strum from his guitar for the flutist. The children were excited with that extra energy we all envy. Their week-long rehearsal had reached an end. They were anxious to celebrate. The culmination of Christmas songs, memorized Bible verses, and the artistic flair of costumes, stage setting, and music any one child could experience or understand. The children worked hard for their presentation of the Christmas Program for their moms and dads.

I walked through the three king's designated zone and entered the kitchen with my plate of cookies. I set them on the counter along with other goodies for the party we'd have after the play.

Leaving the noise and excitement of the classroom, I went outside where the peace and calm of seasonal Christmas carols played through the outdoor intercom. I approached the entry to the sanctuary. Just for a moment, I stopped, took a deep breath, as if I could breathe in some of the Bethlehem fragrances. Evergreen aromas permeated the air and encouraged another deep breath.

Straight in front of me stood two, 10-foot high carved mahogany wooden doors. They were gorgeous and magnificent in strength and beauty, as if they were representative of heaven's glory.

The doors were decorated with large, fresh-cut pine branches, emitting a wonderful scent. Each wreath was adorned with many rainbow colored bulbs and a gold bow. For a split second, my thoughts took me to another time. A time when I will get to meet my Savior on the other side of heaven's double doors.

The doors started to open from the inside. That startled me and brought me back to reality.

As the double doors opened, a hallowed reverence came upon me. I felt the warmth of the Christmas season welcoming me inside. The icicle tea lights draped from the ceiling of the sanctuary projected beautiful light in the magnificent room of white walls and mahogany beam exposure. The glow of imitation candles flickered on the altar and down the inside walls. The golden candelabrum brought a heavenly aura to the chapel. The 15-foot Christmas tree touched the wooden gables in the ceiling and sparkled with white tea lights and silver glass ornaments. The organ softly played Christmas carols.

The audience began to arrive. Grandparents, moms and dads, aunts and uncles, sisters, brothers and friends gathered together and found seats. They, too, shared excitement to see their loved ones participate in the Christmas Story.

Parents, with cameras in hand, moved around to find that just-right place for the perfect picture.

The lights dimmed. Time to start.

Silent Night, started softly. The spotlight panned across the stage as Joseph and Mary knelt in the stable and cradled their baby in the manger. A flutist played *Away in the Manger*.

Kindergarten through second grade children, dressed in angel costumes with wings and halos, moved to center stage and placed themselves where their teacher had previously assigned them. The children stood still while the audience sang, *Oh, Little Town of Bethlehem*. Moms and dads beamed with pride.

The three kings entered the stage from the left. Students, grades three and four, wore their bathrobes and Burger King crowns, covered in aluminum foil. Slowly the kings walked toward the manger. They carried gold, frankincense, and myrrh.

Students, fifth through seventh grade, meandered onto the stage. As the students began to sing and dance to *Joy to the World*, a wonderful rhythm of excitement came forth. The children sang, clapped their hands, danced and used sign language to the carol. They brought real merriment to the celebration of Christ's birth. The audience loved it.

I looked over the children on stage. I found Carlie, a sixth grader, completely enthralled with the joyful music. Uninhibited by those around her, Carlie danced gleefully. She raised her arms over her head portraying the joy she was singing. She moved her feet to the beat. She swayed among her peers and tossed her head upward and smiled with the love of Jesus on her face.

There were only three children in the two- and three-year-old class. When encouraged by their parents or teachers to go up on the stage, one child cried and refused to participate. Another held her mom's hand, then sat down halfway up the steps to the stage. The third child proudly strutted up the three steps to center stage. This three-year-old lass, dressed in her red Christmas dress, took the microphone and waited for her teacher to speak to her.

"Allison, can you tell us the Scripture you memorized last week in Sunday school?"

Allison pursed her little lips on the microphone and with pride and boldness said, "I am fearfully and wonderfully made. Just like baby Jesus."

Most of the quote came from Psalm 139. That said it all. The audience clapped with exuberance and beamed in response to Allison reciting the memory verse.

As all the children returned to the stage for a last applause, I could tell that each thought that they performed their designated part well. The children shared in the celebration of Jesus' birthday through the giving of themselves and had His joy down deep in their hearts.

Later, as I sat by my warm fireplace with a cup of hot tea reflecting over the program, I began to wonder, *Did little Allison understand her quoted Scripture, "I am fearfully and wonderfully made"?*

I remembered the day when my young children practiced and practiced to memorize their Sunday school verses. When did my children truly understand what they were memorizing? I do know seeds were being planted in their hearts, waiting for someone else to water them. Their understanding came with age. Little Allison had a scripture sealed in her heart during this evening's Christmas program. She will always remember that she is "fearfully and wonderfully made." As she grows up she will understand the Scripture more fully as God reveals it to her.

Yes, she stole the show. Not many three-year-old children will go on stage, after a rip roaring dance routine by older peers, and speak into a microphone with a cuddly, soft voice to speak the essence of the season — a baby, and herself, were was fearfully and wonderfully made.

~ *Gayle Fraser*

Attention Shoppers

On Black Friday, I watched shoppers as they fought over the latest, greatest bargains. Grown women and men pulled and tugged in an effort to wrench the much-sought-after deal-of-the-day from the hands of the "lucky" ones.

Wow! Christmas was going to be very good for a select few of those who could fight the hardest, be the toughest, run and jump the fastest and the highest. And those shoppers would go home with not quite as large a bottom line as they would have had if they'd waited to shop another day with their plastic cards.

Announcers added to the hustle and bustle as they encouraged, "Get your blue light special — available for the next two minutes in aisle number five!"

Off shoppers went, hurdling over one another to be the first to grab and claim yet another bargain.

In the midst of the hubbub, my thoughts turned to Jesus Christ. After all, the season is named for him. Instead of the blue light special, I need to keep my primary focus on The Light of the World.

Rather than wrestling some stranger for a bargain that I may not need, I should turn my greatest attention to the One who offered me the best bargain the world has ever known — eternal life.

When future Black Fridays roll around, where will Jesus find me — making my way toward the blue light special or basking in the Light of His Glory and Grace? I could go share the Good News with someone. It's the best Christmas gift anyone could receive, and sharing it will cost absolutely nothing.

What a bargain!

~ Debra DuPree Williams

＋ 50 ＋

One Christmas
Above All Others

B y now I have lived through 85 Christmases, each enjoyable in its own way. But among all of these, my favorite — the one with the deepest meaning — remains the Christmas of 1966 that followed a few days after my return from Vietnam.

The calendar year 1966 was the year of my service in that country. Just before I left the US, my wife Mildred and I had bought a house — the first that we'd owned — in Columbus, Georgia. That's where Mildred and our four children, ages 2 through 11, lived while I was gone. During 1965 we had experienced the personnel turbulence and hurried changes of orders that characterized America's buildup for the Vietnam War. Buying the house gave the family a degree of stability in the midst of that turbulence.

My year in Vietnam eventually passed, and orders came for me to depart to the U.S. on December 20th. At first light that morning I flew one last reconnaissance mission — my personal way of putting an exclamation point at the end of my tour. But five o'clock that afternoon found me dressed in short-sleeved khakis and lined up with hand-carry baggage as a passenger on a chartered flight back to the U.S.

The flight was pleasant and routine. I remember looking down at hundreds of mercury lights as we passed through the darkness over Japan. In Anchorage, Alaska, we passengers had to wait in the airport terminal while the aircraft was refueled. Our short-sleeved khakis were ill suited for the Alaskan winter, so the flight crew issued each of us a blanket. We joked that it looked like the terminal had been invaded by Indians, and a few of the GIs celebrated the occasion with war whoops. A few hours later as we landed in San Francisco, the passengers broke into spontaneous applause.

I found a direct overnight flight to Atlanta, with a connection that would land me at Columbus, Georgia about dawn. The flight into Atlanta was routine, but that last flight into Columbus became a problem — a life-threatening problem.

The aircraft for that short flight was a piston-engine replacement for the classic DC-3. We arrived over Columbus' Muscogee County Airport in the dim light of false dawn, mere moments before sunrise. As the pilot flew southwest on his downwind leg for a visual landing to the northeast, I saw that wisps of fog were forming across the runway. From that height they looked innocent, for we could plainly see the entire runway. But from experience I knew it would be a different story during the last 50 feet of descent to landing. The sun rising behind those wisps of fog would create a blinding glare, a glare so fierce that the pilot could not see enough to land safely.

Nevertheless, our pilot proceeded as if unaware of that condition. As he turned onto final approach, I broke into an angry sweat. And the more we descended, the angrier I became. Had I survived a full tour in Vietnam only to "buy the farm" at my home airport because a foolish civilian pilot chose to fly into a dangerous condition? And at Christmas, too!

Our idiot pilot seemed determined to land regardless of the conditions. Looking out the window, I saw that we were about 30 feet above the ground. The pilot had to be blinded by the glare! I gritted my teeth and assumed the position recommended for a crash — not that it would have done any good.

At the last second, though, the pilot engaged the throttles and made a go-around. He followed that by a routine landing with the sun at his back, as he should have done in the first place. Fortunately for both him and me, he did not leave the pilot's cabin while his passengers deplaned. That saved him from receiving my pointed critique of his intelligence, his decision-making abilities, and probably several more personal matters.

The fog settled in quickly. By the time I got through in the terminal, the visibility was down to about 25 feet. I phoned Mildred that I would take a taxi home. The taxi driver proved more astute than the pilot had been. We crept at snail's pace along the deserted streets. He delivered me safely to our house and received a handsome tip for his efforts. The slow drive through the fog enabled an emotional transition from my anger at the landing, and I emerged into a world quite different from the one I'd known for the past year.

In that moment began the dear moments that made this Christmas special. Mildred welcomed me with a warm embrace. Together, she and I looked in on the children as they slept. I still believe that nothing in this world is as beautiful as a sleeping child. A child's peaceful innocence gives us the merest glance of something like Eden must have been.

Mildred and I then drank morning coffee and caught up on news since our last contact. We let the children awaken one by one, each making an individual discovery that Daddy was home. Each one climbed onto my lap for a hug and an individual catch-up conversation. After their breakfast I spent the morning admiring their latest drawings and the schoolwork they were proud of, and listening to their interests.

Over the next few days, Mildred and I arranged for Santa to bring things the children could carry to Europe for our next assignment. In the backs of our minds, we knew that much had to be done toward that move. We had 30 days to sell the house, sell one car and deliver the other to port for shipment, divide the household goods for shipment within the weight limit with the rest going into storage — and there would be dozens of other, unforeseen details. We also knew that personnel turbulence and reorganizations within the U.S. Seventh Army would make our European tour labor-intensive.

But for now we pushed all that into the background. For the present, it was enough for the family to be together again, to rest in our love for each other and, in the quiet of our home, in that special ambience T.S. Eliot termed "the still point of the turning world," to celebrate the birth of our Lord, who is The One Answer to all the churning evils of the world.

Through the many years since then, the golden glow of that homecoming Christmas remains in my memory as a time of the deepest peace and pleasure that life can afford.

~ Donn Taylor

Christmas Eve Vigil

M om-Mom, I hear him," I whispered, sitting up in bed. With the covers sliding off, I leaned toward the other twin bed where my grandmother slept, or tried to, during my all-night vigil watching for Santa. Cool air touched my skin, but my excitement warmed me. "I hear something on the roof."

I still recall the sweet scent of her beauty-salon hairdo, as she shook her head and whispered for me to go to sleep or Santa couldn't come visit our house. Mom-Mom stayed overnight every Christmas Eve. It was a family tradition. I was no more than five at the time, but the memories of that dark night have never faded. I knew Santa was out there, somewhere, nearby, and likely to sweep in close when I wasn't looking. I believed Santa knew I had been good all year.

Deeper in the night, I looked over and thought I saw my grandmother, appearing to be sitting upright in a rocking chair. When I woke her to tell her that, she wasn't pleased.

"Robin, please go to sleep." She still whispered, but with an edge to her voice now. "You're trying too hard. You know he'll be here."

I tried to comply, I really did. I could then perceive that she was indeed lying down, not sitting in a chair. But as I lay there, staring into blackness, my belief grew stronger that Santa was with me, and could be on our roof at any time, whether or not I could see or hear him.

Most children in our country are lucky, and will have their beliefs confirmed on Christmas morning. As we mature, we concentrate more on the celebration of Christmas being about the birth of Jesus, the one to whom we are accountable.

Jesus knows who has been naughty and who has been nice.

When we fear, or worry, or stare into long moments of blackness, we need to keep the childlike wonder fresh with anticipation, knowing that not only can our Lord be on our roof at any time, but better than that, God is available to be with us every day, in our hearts. And that is the beauty of Jesus being the reason for Christmas.

– Robin Bayne

Santa's Mishap

I stood at our dining room window staring at the falling snow. What I saw was disheartening. "Mom, it's snowing so hard. How will Santa see our house with all the snow filling up the sky?" My eight-year-old mind was worried. "Even Rudolph couldn't see through this."

Mother came in from the kitchen, wiping cookie dough off her hands. She stood next to me staring at the huge flakes. "It's supposed to stop after lunch time. Why don't you call Jane and Cindy and see if they want to go sledding on Dalton's hill? All this fresh snow is sure to make your sleds go fast."

"Okay, but I'm not going to stop worrying." I turned from the window with my shoulders slumped. I walked over to the wall phone to call my best friends. Maybe they were worrying too.

Hours later I came home with wet mittens and rosy cheeks. I put my snow-drenched double knit mittens on the drying rack my mother put over the heating vent in the dining room floor. They would be warm and dry in no time.

"Oh good, you're back!" Mom said as I followed the scrumptious scent of her famous chocolate chip cookies baking in the oven. "Just in time for lunch."

Knowing she worked hard to make our Christmas special, I smiled as I took a seat at the kitchen table. "The snow is stopping. Santa should be here right on time tonight, right Mom?"

She placed a grilled cheese sandwich and two cookies on my plate. "Sandwich first!" she said as I reached for a cookie, still warm from the oven.

Mom sighed. "I need to talk about Santa's arrival tonight."

"Why?" I asked with a mouth full of cheese. If I ate the sandwich quickly I could get to those cookies.

She ignored the rule about never talking with a mouth full of food. "This year will be different than last Christmas Eve."

My shoulders drooped and my bottom lip stuck out. "You have to work tomorrow, huh?"

Mother was a nurse at the hospital in our small city. The nurses rotated work schedules on the holidays. I was used to it, but still...Christmas Day? Who would roast the turkey and mash the potatoes?

"Yes, I have to work. So, earlier this month I wrote a letter to Santa and asked if he could start with our house on his trip around the world."

My eyes got really big. "You did?"

"I did. He didn't answer, but I'm hoping he starts here. Maybe he will come when you're at your grandparents after church tonight. Your dad's going to take you."

"Aren't you coming with us?"

"I have to get cooking done for tomorrow."

Well, that explained who would cook Christmas dinner.

After lunch I went upstairs to my bedroom and read the story about the birth of Jesus. I wondered if Mary and Joseph had to travel through snow on their long journey to Bethlehem.

Later, Mom knocked on my door. Her hands were behind her and I knew she was holding a present. She always gave me a special present every year on Christmas Eve afternoon. I think it was to keep me occupied while waiting for the Christmas Eve service at church, and for the magic hour when Santa would arrive. I quickly unwrapped it. "Wow, Mom, a Paint by Numbers! I love this."

Mom smiled. I jumped off the bed and wrapped my arms around her waist. "You're the best mom a kid could ever have."

I spent the rest of the afternoon at the dining room table. I had the canvas, the paints, the little brush, a small dish of water and an old rag all laid out before me. I got right to work on my masterpiece. Before I knew it, the sun had set and it was dark outside. My dad came into the room and admired my painting. "Nice job there, kiddo."

"Thanks, Dad. I worked really, really hard on it. Some day when I'm grown up I'm going to be a real artist and paint my own pictures."

"I have no doubt you will. But for now, you need to pick this stuff up, get washed, and change your clothes for church."

"Are we going to Grandma's house too? Do we have to stay long? Santa might be coming early tonight and I don't want to miss him."

"We'll be home in plenty of time, don't you worry."

I put my partially done painting away and ran upstairs to my bedroom to change clothes. Mom had laid out my Christmas dress, tights and new shiny black leather shoes on the bed. I felt pretty and festive wearing them. When I was done primping for the evening ahead, I walked down the stairs like a model on a fashion runway. My parents were waiting for me in the living room.

Dad turned to Mom. "Who is this beautiful young lady standing before us?"

Mom shrugged. "Why, I have no idea. She does look familiar though."

I covered my mouth and giggled. "It's me, you sillies."

"Oh, we didn't recognize you in your Christmas outfit." We all enjoyed laughing about that.

I was excited about the Christmas Eve service at church. I loved the carols we sang and that our priest had the children sit with him on the altar steps as he read from the Bible about the birth of Jesus. Before taking our seats we placed a wrapped canned food item in the basket to the side of the altar railing. It simulated the gifts the wise men brought to the Christ child. Our gift would go to families in need.

The service ended with the choir leading us in singing "Silent Night" as they walked down the aisle two by two. The doors of the church opened. Our priest, Father Neal, stood in the doorway on that cold and snowy night shaking everyone's hand and wishing us all a very blessed Christmas.

"*Okay, one down, one to go,*" I thought as Dad brushed off a new coating of snow from the windows of our car. I shivered, willing the heater to bring warm air to my body. The ride to my grandparents' house was slow. Snow was piling up on the roads at a fast pace.

I looked at Dad. "I hope we can make the hill to Grandma's house without getting stuck."

"I'll get a good start and we'll make it right into the driveway."

I wasn't too sure about that but I kept my mouth shut and watched the snowflakes come directly at us like pellets. I wondered how he could see to drive. I guessed he must be a pro at this because he was as cool as a cucumber behind the wheel. Soon we turned onto Grandma's street and sure enough, he gunned that engine and the old car took off. We arrived in the driveway right on time.

I loved going to my grandparents' for Christmas Eve. We got hugs from Grandma after we took off our wet coats and boots and hung them in the entryway. My grandfather and my aunt were waiting for us in the living room.

"How was church?" Grandpa asked as we ate the traditional dinner of pot roast, potatoes, carrots and homemade bread, still warm. Oh, and sauerkraut, always sauerkraut. I loved listening to my grandpa's subtle German accent.

"It was so nice." I answered, still basking in the glow of all those candles, the Christmas hymns, and the crèche on the altar.

They were all smiles as we passed the bowls and platters of food around while I described the church service. I wished Mom could be with us, but understood she had to get things ready for Christmas dinner at our house tomorrow.

After what seemed like hours of opening gifts, and adult conversations, it was time to leave. We said our goodbyes, gave hugs and got back in the car.

"There's a lot more snow on the road now," Dad said.

"I sure hope Santa can find our house in all this snow."

"He hasn't missed a year yet, has he?"

"Now that I think about it, you're right." I felt a little better, but snow was piling up. "Dad, do you know if Mary and Joseph had to travel through snowstorms on their way from Nazareth?"

"The Bible doesn't mention anything about that."

Still wondering about it I sat back in my seat as Dad slowly but surely made the long trek back home. Finally, he turned into our driveway at the side of the house. I opened the car door two seconds after he turned off the engine. The snow was higher than the top of my boots, so I gingerly walked to our back door. "I really appreciate the path you are caving out" Dad said and smiled as I grabbed his gloved hand. We walked into the kitchen, glad to be home. The house seemed empty and eerily quiet.

"Where's Mom?" I asked.

Then I heard someone or something slowly coming up the basement stairs. My heart was thumping. I grabbed Dad's hand and moved closer to him. He looked down at me and shrugged, baffled by the unfamiliar movement behind the closed basement door.

Suddenly the doorknob rattled back and forth. There was a muffled sound like paper rustling. I stood frozen in place. My brave dad moved toward the basement door. Neither of us made a sound.

Just as Dad reached for the knob, the door flew open. Dad jumped back. I screamed. Frightened, I hid behind Dad.

He began laughing so hard his body shook. I peeked around him and couldn't believe my eyes. There in the doorway stood my mom with her arms full of wrapped presents.

Mom peered at us around the tall stack of presents. She held them with both hands and seemed at a loss for words. It was as though she got caught doing something she didn't want us to see.

"You would not believe what happened," she said in a melodramatic way. She put the packages on the kitchen floor and plunked down in a chair. She then proceeded to explain this unexpected dilemma.

"I heard Santa's sleigh land on the roof," she began. "Then I heard his footsteps walk to the chimney. I hid in the kitchen so he wouldn't see me. Santa doesn't like to be seen when he comes down the chimney and puts the presents under the tree." She paused, then continued. "Anyway, the next sound I heard was a clunk and a crash. I thought the furnace was acting up again. I quickly peeked at the Christmas tree, but there was no sign of Santa anywhere. I was so sure he came down the chimney. Suddenly I heard a loud moaning coming from the basement. I ran to the stairs, yanked the door open and turned on the light. I hollered, 'Who's down there?'"

I hung onto Mom's every word. "What happened next?"

"Yes, dear. I'm dying to know how this story ends." Dad gave me a conspiratorial wink.

"So," Mom continued, "I went down the basement stairs. When I reached the bottom step I couldn't believe my eyes. There was Santa, sprawled on the floor, covered in soot."

Mom looked straight at Dad. "By the way, it would have been considerate if you had cleaned the chimney for Santa's arrival. Imagine my embarrassment."

Concerned, I asked, "Was Santa hurt?"

"No, he's so roly-poly he enjoyed that little tumble and said he wasn't thinking about the chimney going all the way to the basement and he missed the living room. I helped him clean the soot off his suit and gather the presents. He asked me if I would take them upstairs and put them under the tree. He was running late and the snowstorm was slowing him down. I was happy to help him. After all, he *is* Santa Claus. I thanked him for the presents. He stood at the chimney and with this finger beside his nose. With a nod of his head, he was gone. Just like that." She spread her hands. "End of story."

I realized I had just missed him. I almost couldn't believe that really happened, but there's a certain magic in Christmas and a joy that comes from having childlike wonder during the season.

Each Christmas Eve I've thought of the story my mother told us. I guess you could say she was truly one of Santa's elves that memorable, and never-to-be-forgotten Christmas Eve in 1957.

~ *Cathy Ancewicz*

✦ 53 ✦
Display of Lights

Who among you fears the LORD and obeys the word of his servant?
Let the one who walks in the dark, who has no light,
trust in the name of the LORD and rely on their God.
Isaiah 50:10 (NIV)

Lights. We love lights, especially Christmas lights. We hang strands of lights around our mantles, up and over our porches, and drape our tree with more than the fire marshal allows.

We drive miles to see the most decorated houses in town or out-of-town. From Anderson, South Carolina's two-and-a-half million lights, Clifton, Ohio's three-and-a-half million, or through Buford, Georgia's seven miles of shimmering ones, we seek the lights.

We deck halls, streets, racetracks, and parks. The more-lights-the-better is a worldwide obsession. In 2011, an Australian couple strung 97,211 feet of Christmas lights and won the Guinness Record for the most residential lights.

What is it about lights?

We seek light because we're created in the image of God. Yes, we're attracted to artificial light because it's helpful, lovely, and because light is imprinted into our being.

The Bible tells us God is light and there is no darkness in him. In fact, God's light is brilliant — so brilliant there's no need of a sun where he lives. His eyes flame like fire and his feet gleam like burnished bronze. Yet he created the sun to provide warmth and light for Earth. When Jesus lived on Earth, he told the people he was the light of the world. Real light comes from seeking Jesus. We seek him through Bible reading and prayer.

Sometimes I wonder how I'm going to live without my Christmas lights all year, but the end of the Christmas season doesn't mean the end of light. This year when it's time to disassemble the tree, pull down the lights, and box everything away, don't feel gloomy. We don't have to live without light.

The life-changing everlasting light, from our Mighty God, our wonderful counselor, our Prince of Peace, will shine through us.

For me, I've found that seeking advice from people, rather than reading the Bible, led me down dark paths. In my past I listened to friends, and yes, even family, who told me what I wanted to hear, instead of giving me biblical advice. I made mistakes, and many of those decisions affect my life on a daily basis. Now, any advice I hear must align with God's word or I reject it. When I'm unsure, I continue to pray.

How do we focus on the God's light instead of the flashy lifestyle the world offers us that doesn't include God? We begin by trusting God, sticking with him, even when we can't see what lies ahead.

We don't have to drive for miles to find Jesus. Start praying. He hears us wherever we are. When we turn to the Bible we find timeless advice.

Our Christmas lights are artificial. The real light is from God. When we practice seeking the real light and seeing the results, we'll begin to crave God's light.

What a joy to read Bible verses such as Genesis 1:27, Isaiah 9: 6–7, 1 John 1:5, Revelation 1:12-15, and Revelation 21:23, pray, and experience the truth.

We can trust the Light of our World.

~ Terri Kelly

54

The Christmas Santa Died and Rudolph Became Toast

When I first had my doubts about there being a Santa Claus, and wondering if my parents might be outright lying to me about the big jolly fat man, I began sleuth-snooping.

It started when my older siblings let the cat out of the box when a large rectangular package arrived on our front porch, delivered by the mailman while we were on Christmas break and our parents were at work. One of the traitorous siblings — the one who was six years older than me — suggested we cut a small hole in the cardboard so we could feel around inside to see what secrets might be tugged out.

Since my hand was tiniest — and probably so they could blame me should anything go wrong and we were found out — it was decided that my fingers would be the ones to do the surreptitious probing.

When I pulled out a small, chunky, brown plastic chair, I realized the box held a dollhouse. But...a chunky, brown chair? That was not the same dollhouse that had been on my Santa Claus list.

My siblings laughed.

All I could think about was that Santa couldn't get anything right, and besides, this was proof he wasn't real.

In all fairness, I'll leave Daddy out of this because Mother did all of the Christmas shopping. Now, *she* couldn't even be counted on to pull through for *that* job...and if Mother — smart and always capable — couldn't be depended on to get Santa business right, how could I depend on God? Was he not real either? If he was real, couldn't he have intervened when Santa... cough...Mother...chose my dollhouse?

Bah humbug! Not only was Santa not real, it was evident that Mother had ordered the dollhouse through a mail order catalog, because the chunky brown chair was the ugliest chair I'd ever seen.

While my siblings laughed at the chair and my bad luck, I gnashed my teeth and inwardly wailed. I couldn't put a name on it at the time because I was only seven, but I felt forsaken.

Everything else I touched with my hand through the box's hole was too big to free and would only make the hole much larger if I kept tugging. My siblings ordered me to cease and desist. They didn't want to incur Santa's wrath or make Mother suspicious that she'd been found out. They wanted to pretend Santa was real for as long as they could for fear some of the presents beneath the tree would be curtailed if it was suspected they knew the truth.

I kept voting to make the hole larger, however, my siblings said absolutely not. "No way are you spoiling Christmas!" They were of the same consensus, however, that the dollhouse chair was the ugliest brown chair they'd ever laid eyes on.

At least we agreed on something.

The next two weeks were the longest weeks of my life. Christmas was ruined for me. Filled with disappointment, I pretended all was well. I acted like decorating the tree was fun. I tried to enjoy watching the tree's bubble lights but they didn't seem quite as beautiful as they had in previous years. I was only in second grade without too many holidays under my belt.

So the snooper-sleuth faked it.

When Daddy put Santa in his sleigh pulled by reindeer on the rooftop — to be all lit up for the Christmas gawkers — and asked me to assist in holding some of the lights for him, I felt like shouting to my neighborhood friends who were helping their parents decorate outside, "Hey you guys, it's all a sham — one big huge lie. There is no Fat Man! Santa Claus is a farce! Let me repeat! There is no Santa Claus! Santa is dead, which means Rudolph is toast! And my Mother has the worst taste in the world when it comes to choosing dollhouses!"

But of course, I kept my mouth shut, because if I had convinced the doubters I was right, the younger kids in the neighborhood would have been squalling that there was no Santa; therefore no presents from Santa. I'd be the worst kid on the block and my friends would ostracize me forever for spoiling Christmas.

If all of these new revelations weren't enough trauma for a kid in elementary school, licking the spoon clean of its cake batter when Mother baked Christmas cakes wasn't such a treat anymore either. Knowing what I was going to get for Christmas was now a bummer. No surprises in the near future, really, since the dollhouse would be my "big" gift. And worst of all, the dollhouse wasn't even going to be a dainty feminine dollhouse; it was obviously going to be decorated with man-cave furniture. At that tender age, I was more of a shabby chic kind of kid when it came to my dolls and doodads.

The only conclusion I could wrap my little mind around having to do with all of this travesty was that Mother loved brown. She'd always dressed my sister in brown — which sis hated — because Mother thought brown dresses accentuated brown eyes.

But I was my own person. I hated brown anything unless it had something to do with chocolate, horses, or dogs.

What in the world was Santa…er…Mother…thinking?

Finally, the climactic morning of the Big Lie rolled around. I dragged myself out of bed to face what was beneath the tree. Once in the living room, I braced myself to be repulsed.

But lo and behold, there in front of me as I rubbed my sleepy eyes, was the most darling dollhouse I'd ever seen. Sure, the ugly chunky brown chair was there, but it was surrounded by blue and pink beautifully arranged furniture that complimented the wallpaper. The ugly brown chair didn't seem so ugly anymore when placed in its gorgeous surroundings.

With a new sense of excitement along with jingle bell thrills, I later realized I'd done all of that worrying for nothing. I'd experienced so much doom and gloom leading up to the celebration of the birth of Christ — the real reason for the season — when I could have been rejoicing with gladness all along because I not only had a Savior, I had a pretty cool fake Santa and Rudolf on the rooftop and in the kitchen there were plenty of wooden spoons to lick!

I didn't have everything I wanted, but I had just what I needed — enough.

It wouldn't be until many years later, when I reflected back over my life and my many Jesus moments that I realized contemporary people aren't much different than the ancients when it comes to God's bailouts and surprises.

God always came through at the last minute in olden days so he could teach people to trust him throughout their life journeys while building faith and hope in him.

I discovered that God is always there, even during those last minutes when I think I'll be overrun by chariots and horse hooves before my sea parts. And He'll always be there, unless it's my appointed time to be taken home.

In taking a closer look at some of the Bible stories, I've gained a new understanding of God's timing.

When it seemed that Abram wouldn't get the heir he was promised, God stepped in at the last minute — during Abraham's golden years — and blessed him with a son. More than one.

When Job's troubles were horrendous and he thought death might be forthcoming, he was healed and given additional children and renewed wealth to replace what he'd lost.

The Red Sea parted at the last minute, when the Israelites thought all was lost.

And Jesus cried out from the cross, "My God my God, why have you forsaken me?" The death of Jesus was necessary so mankind could be redeemed through him.

Even though I couldn't see what else was in store for me from the box dropped off on my front porch so many years ago — and I still don't know what my future holds — God has known all along what he has planned for me and he delights in the many gifts he's freely given and still freely gives.

Evidently, God loves delighting his children with surprises, though sometimes in my case my heart flutters during the anticipation.

Even if I never receive another gift from Santa and his elves — or from family members or friends — I've already received the greatest gift of all: Jesus Christ. What a gift he truly is.

Knowing that even if there might be a chunky brown chair in my mansion in heaven when I get there, because Jesus has promised me a mansion, I won't mind. In fact, I've grown to love the color brown — the same color that enhanced my once-dark eyes that eventually turned hazel.

And to this day I truly feel blessed.

~ *Vicki H. Moss*

55

Through the Eyes of a Child

The clock read 5:36 a.m. I had four minutes until the dreadful sound of the alarm would go off. Everything in me wanted to stay snuggled under the covers but there was work to be done. With one eye open and flashlight in hand, I made my way to my daughter's room where I pried Mittens, the elf, out of her arms. I then gathered up Christopher, my son's elf, and stood there asking "What shenanigans can these crazy rascals get into this morning?"

Thirty minutes later, Ava peeked from around the corner and asked in a soft tone with a slight lisp the same question she had for days, "Where's Mittens?" Soon, their scavenger hunt began as they ran from room to room with anticipation of what they would find. Moments later I heard my favorite sound on the planet. Both of my little ones chuckled as they discovered their bathroom covered in toilet paper and the two elves sitting ever so innocently on the towel rack.

In the middle of that normal Thursday morning, after I made sure teeth were brushed, hair was combed and bags were packed, for just a brief moment, I was able to forget my responsibilities and return to a childlike frame of mind while the three of us had a good giggle. Oh, to be young again! Where simplicity, innocence and belief seem to be intertwined.

With Christmas upon us, a sense of wonder and enchantment fills the air. It's a time of hope, of giving, and when mischievous elves have daring adventures no eye has seen. Santa is able to deliver toys to every little boy and girl, if they're on the good list of course. To see and experience this season through a child's eyes is quite magical.

Is it possible that we adults can bring ourselves to a childlike state not only at Christmas but year round? Matthew 18:2-5 (MSG) tells us: Whoever becomes simple and elemental again, like this child, will rank high in God's kingdom.

That doesn't mean to act immaturely but rather to have the complete trust of a young child and to believe in the unseen. Children are the best examples of meekness and are teachable. We must take God at his word with reverence and simplicity, and humble ourselves before the Lord. Ephesians 5:1 (NLT) tells us: Follow God's example in everything you do, because you are his dear children.

God is love. Who, but children, better represents unconditional love like our Father?

As exciting as it is to carry on traditions, hang stockings and wrap presents, there would be no cause to celebrate had it not been for the birth of a babe who lowly entered this world. Jesus, in all his holiness, has taught us the way to live.

May we constantly seek our Savior, Jesus Christ in eager expectancy of the joy he brings. As we marvel at our own offspring may we strive to be more like children.

~ *Dianna Owens*

✦ 56 ✦

Let All the Earth Rejoice!

Rejoice greatly, O my people! Shout with joy!
For look — your King is coming! He is the Righteous One, the Victor!
Zechariah 9:9 TLB

Night unfolds its veil of darkness across the light of day. Shimmering constellations pale as one bright star sets the ebony sky ablaze. Flocks lie still, serene in the field.

Shepherds gather around a flickering fire to dispel the evening chill. Only the calming crackle of the fire breaks the silence.

Suddenly, the radiance of an angel of the Lord rips open the night's veil. The shepherds fall on their faces, trembling. The angel reassures this band of quaking caretakers, "Do not be afraid. I bring you good news of great joy that will be for all the people. Today in the town of David a Savior has been born to you; He is Christ the Lord" (Luke 2:10-11 NIV).

The darkness erupts into a brilliant glory as a chorus of angels bursts forth to proclaim a Divine Appearance: "Glory to God in the highest, and on earth peace, goodwill toward men!" (Luke 2:14 NKJV).

In the distance, a newborn's cry pervades the cool, night air with new life. The King of heaven has bowed low, entering earth's time capsule. The Babe Jesus — dressed in a suit of humanity — arrives, just as Isaiah prophesied:

For unto us a Child is born,
Unto us a Son is given;
And the government will be upon His shoulder.
And His name will be called
Wonderful, Counselor, Mighty God,
Everlasting Father, Prince of Peace.
Of the increase of His government and peace
There will be no end.
Isaiah 9:6-7a NKJV

Mary said, "My soul magnifies the Lord, and my spirit has rejoiced in God my Savior" (Luke 1:46-47 NKJV). Are you in agreement with Mary?

Maybe your soul is suffering this year. Maybe you have lost a loved one. Maybe divorce has ripped your family apart. Maybe your best friend has deserted you. Maybe your child is out of a job or has gotten into trouble. Maybe foreclosure is knocking at your door.

Whatever the trial, join in with Mary.

Rejoice at Jesus' birth!

Rejoice He came to save the world.

Rejoice He prepared you an Eternal Home.

Let your soul magnify the Lord, and your spirit rejoice in the Babe of the manger this season.

Jehovah is King! Let all the earth rejoice!

Psalm 97:1 TLB

~ Lynn Mosher

57

Bicycles for Christmas

A bicycle for Christmas! What child hasn't dreamed of one? And what fun it is for the grown-ups who plan the surprise for the child.

We whispered and kept secrets for months the year we got a bicycle for Bill, our five-year-old son. He would be so proud to have his first "big" bike. We found a second-hand one in good condition. "He will never know it isn't new," we assured ourselves. "It will clean up just fine."

My mother was as excited as my husband and I were. "Hide it at our house," she said. "It's a long time until Christmas, but your secret will be safe here."

While Bill was in kindergarten and his older sisters at school, Mother and I scrubbed and cleaned off every smudge. Then we headed to the store for a can of bright blue paint. We took special care to make sure not even a tiny blue spatter got on the shiny chrome. When it looked as bright as we could get it, we sneaked it from Mother's house to ours and buried it under the hay in the hayloft.

How anxiously my husband and I waited for Christmas morning! Bill would be so excited when he saw his bike!

Just as we expected, he loved it.

But we weren't the only ones who kept secrets that year. Our son and his four sisters either did not want to spoil our surprise or they were afraid to admit they had snooped. Whatever the reason, those five kids never said a word. They kept quiet for 20 years until one Christmas, as young adults, they reminisced around our Christmas tree.

"Remember when we found Bill's bike hidden in the hayloft?" one of the girls asked. They laughed as they told us how they'd all climbed the stairs to the loft and ridden the bike. We adults would have been scared out of our wits if we'd known what those kids were doing in that open loft.

Our family enjoyed our second Christmas bicycle surprise when the kids were close to the teen years. That was the year they all got brand new bicycles. An unexpected check in November covered the cost for a mass purchase, and my husband and I went shopping to pick out five ten-speeds.

The young clerk who wheeled out bike after bike couldn't hide her amazement. She'd stop on her way through the store and ask fellow-clerks, "Can you believe this? Look how many bicycles they bought."

When Christmas Eve came, it took some late-night sneakiness to smuggle five shiny new bicycles into the house while five kids whispered behind their closed doors. We heard their giggles, but none of them dared to venture out of their rooms. After we lined the bikes wall-to-wall in the living room, we turned off the lights and went to bed.

We spent a restless night, too tense to sleep. The next morning, we hurried out of our room. Our kids were always early risers on Christmas morning. We couldn't miss their reactions at the sight awaiting them. All five rushed through the house, and then they stopped short and stared. That time they hadn't snooped. They were absolutely amazed.

My husband planned the last bicycle Christmas at our house, but it wasn't for the kids. He decided to give me one...and by that time I was a gray-haired grandma. He worked for hours in the evenings to get my old one-speed cleaned and repaired.

On Christmas morning, it was our kids and grandkids who watched and waited to see what I'd do. Self-conscious to be the one with a two-wheeler propped under the tree, I barely managed a weak thank-you to my husband.

My husband and I had no idea of the bicycle memories we would build through the years. That long-ago day when we found a good-as-new used bike for our son was the beginning. He and I never dreamed a few years later we would successfully hide five new ten-speeds from the eyes of five snooping kids. And the final surprise, over a quarter century later, was another rejuvenated model. The kids had had their turn. Now it was time for this grandma to ride again. Our bicycle Christmases had come full circle.

- LeAnn Campbell

58

Jen's Annual Cookie Swap

On the back cover of an old cookbook is a photo I've taped there. No one saw me take it and the value is mine alone. I close my eyes and that moment in time, depicted in the photo, comes alive in my memory:

> It is that time of year again, Jen's Annual Cookie Swap. The faithful friends and family willing to endure my strict rules (nothing store bought) are walking through the front door. Soon my home is filled with happy noise. My sister is laughing. My friend Barb is carrying a large wrapped grab bag that looks and smells suspiciously like an evergreen wreath. I know there will be a fight for that one. Another friend is gathering coats. The air still smells like hundreds of freshly baked sugar cookies. Soon we'll sit down to decorate. Hot chocolate is steaming on the stove and the fridge is stocked with extra whipped cream. Chatter is all around me. I hear lots of "I want that recipe" and "so good to see you." There is honest-to-goodness peace and joy. We swap our cookies and begin traditions.
>
> It's cold outside as we bundle up to go caroling. Snow is blowing everywhere as we head down the street to begin our serenades. After singing off-key Christmas songs at a handful of homes, we stop last at my next-door neighbor's house. She is terminally ill. Our singing moves both her and her husband to tears. We give them cookies and he tries to pay us $50, which makes us laugh despite our heavy hearts. We give hugs and head back to the house to start the cookie-decorating contest.
>
> When everyone is sitting at the table frosting cookies, I feel inexplicably led to take a photo. So I do.

I open my eyes and smile even though I feel tears rolling down my face. So much has changed. Some in the photo are no longer here. I didn't know it then, but it would be my last cookie swap. A job transfer soon sent me 1,000 miles away. I taped the picture on my cookbook as a reminder of a Christmas filled with the joy of giving.

What I remember almost every Christmastime is the promise and the hope. No matter where we are or what life holds, Christmas is Christmas. Showing the light and sharing the love keeps the memories forever held in our hearts.

Just close your eyes and see.

To help, I'll even share a recipe.

Sugar Cookies

Ingredients:

3 cups flour
2 ½ teaspoons baking powder
1 ½ cups sugar
2 tablespoons milk or cream
⅔ cup shortening
1 ½ teaspoons vanilla
2 eggs
½ teaspoon salt
My Secret Ingredient: The zest from one orange

Instructions:

Mix all ingredients together. Shape into a ball and refrigerate for a couple of hours. When ready to roll out (¼ inch thickness) and cut into shapes, preheat the oven to 400 degrees. Bake 8 minutes. Cool and frost with your favorite icing. Decorate! Enjoy!

- Jen Waldron

59

The Man in the Red Suit

For 45 years, I've been there, with the exception of a couple years when I lived out of state. Even on those Christmases when I couldn't get back, my heart was warmed by thoughts of my cousins, aunts, and uncles filling the big purple family room on those cold December days.

Now, it isn't uncommon for there to be 100 people or more, none further apart than third cousins, with new little ones every year — all because two teenagers went a-courtin' decades ago in Celina, Ohio farm country, romancing each other in the marching band and on an ice-skating pond.

The family has grown, and the house has changed over the years, but despite temporary tiffs, rivalries, and skirmishes that affect all families, what has never changed is the love that knits us all together.

Christmas memories are forever cherished, like soft patches in the comfortable quilt of our lives. At the root of most of my memories are my grandparents, two of the most spectacular people I've ever known. Truly, I could hold a grudge if I wanted to, considering that my grandpa accidentally ruined the mystique of Santa Claus for me.

When the man in the red suit showed up at our house on Christmas Eve in the early 70s, I wondered (and asked) why he was wearing Grandpa's wristwatch. It was painful to discover that Santa is not real, but now, older and wiser, I realize that instead of destroying Santa for me, Grandpa has spent his lifetime showing me the beauty of being one.

He had humble beginnings, and as a young man, dedicated to becoming a Baptist preacher, he had a wife and family to feed and only seven cents in his pocket. He is part of that rare breed quickly going extinct, the kind of man who is always willing to work hard, to be thankful to his Maker for every provision, and to pass blessings on to anyone in any way he can. My grandma is the same way, and when I look at her beloved Precious Moments collection, I have to smile, because the reality is my grandparents have been the reason many people have experienced miraculous, life-changing, precious moments of their own.

Each Christmas, we gather around Grandma and Grandpa Miesse. Their generous gifts are handed out to their children and grandchildren. The huge stockpot of flappers, a chicken-dumpling-like recipe passed down from my great-grandma and made by my aunt and uncle, fills the kitchen with a wonderful aroma. Pies and the bread cubes for Grandpa's famous oyster dressing line the counters.

The younger children huddle in various sections of the house, giggling at their inside jokes and showing off their new gadgets. The adults and older kids reminisce about life before all those gadgets, and Christmas carries on with laughter, conversation, talented fingers dancing over the ivories of Grandma's baby grand, and lots of catching up with people we enjoy but don't see often enough, separated by miles and busyness throughout the year.

In 2014, though, our focus was not on the tree. It was not on the gifts, not on the feast. It was not on the new clothes we'd unwrapped that morning, not on the icy weather or the football games. We didn't talk about it much, because it was too grim to bring up, but that year, our minds were on another day — a day in January — when we would learn if that great man, our own Santa, would have to be cut open by a surgeon in an attempt to repair one of the biggest hearts ever owned by a human being.

The flappers continued boiling behind us. The tree lights twinkled in the living room. The wind blew beyond the bay window, combing over the yard where I'd played on summer days as a little girl. But in that moment, in that room, all was truly calm and bright.

The children quieted, and we all bowed our heads. Gathered there in a tearful, loving cluster around my grandparents, we prayed as a family — and not just a good-bread-good-meat-good-God-let's-eat kind of prayer. The braver ones shared their prayers out loud. The weepier, shyer ones like me offered silent but heartfelt petitions. Never had the house been so quiet on Christmas day, and never had I felt such closeness and love with my family as we all asked God, in our own way, "Your will be done, Lord…but please let us keep Grandpa a little longer."

When the praying stopped, Grandpa smiled at us. "Grandma and I have had a great life," he said, "and we've been able to share it with all of you. If it's my time to go, I'll leave a light on for ya so you can find me up there, but there is one thing we want. Just love each other. Love the Lord and love other people in every way you can. If you all do that, we'll know we've taught you right."

In that moment, I thought back to a week earlier, when my daughter and I had driven my old 1997 Corolla to the seedier part of town, to a bus stop. We'd left a small package there on a lonely bench, a little wrapped box with a poem and a ten-dollar gift card in it, our way of telling a stranger that Someone above cares about them. It wasn't much, but it was what I could afford at the time, and we hoped it would provide someone a warm meal on a chilly night.

Through my tears on Christmas morning, I looked at my grandpa and realized it was exactly the kind of thing they have always done, giving to and loving kin and strangers alike, in their everyday lives, their ministry, and the health business to which they dedicated 40-plus years.

A few Fridays later, my grandpa lay on a table beneath a scalpel. The prayers for him were many, but we had to face the reality that we could lose him, that God could call him home to that big woodshop in the sky. Like any proper Santa, Grandpa loves making wooden toys and has always said we'll find him at the end of the sawdust trail up there.

God was gracious, though, and Grandpa is still with us today. This past Christmas, a year later, he was sitting right there in that living room with us as my cousin Sydney read the Christmas story from the old black Bible. His health is not great, but the surgeons who worked on him last year said he is somewhat of a miracle.

I couldn't agree more.

We never know how many more Christmases we'll be able to spend with our loved ones, but to me, Grandpa will always be the man in the red suit, because he gives the perfect gift of love in every way he can. He never forgets that it all started in a manger, and he wants all of us to remember that, too, even when God does take him home.

~ Autumn J. Conley

Author's note: My grandparents (whom this story is about) love Operation Christmas Child. After their home was damaged in a house fire, they had a huge yard/estate sale and gave All of the proceeds to Samaritan's Purse.

Wise Men Still Seek Him

Walking through Hobby Lobby, I browsed through the Christmas collectibles, drawn to the ones that show the wise men. Above one painting were the words, "Wise Men Still Seek Him."

I was reminded of the Christmas Passion Plays my family attended. After the birth of the Christ child, three wise men and their entourage journeyed to pay homage to the Holy Babe. I have seen a variety of re-enactments, ranging from live camels, to real samples of gold, myrrh and frankincense, and to banners that declare the various names of God.

However, my favorite Passion Play goes a step further. Once the wise men have made their entry, they are followed by common people of today. Those often include a nurse, teacher, businessman, policeman, fireman, member of the military, and concludes with the entry of Santa Claus.

The contemporary characters kneel among the wise men to worship the Holy Babe. At the conclusion, one of the Wise Men tenderly takes the child from his mother's arm and lifts him toward heaven.

These people of today entering along with the Wise Men to pay homage to the Christ Child is a reminder that even today God is saying, as in the words of the song, "*O Come All Ye Faithful.*" Even today God wants us to come to Him, follow Him and be faithful to Him. So how do we do this?

This is done first by surrendering our hearts and lives to Him. A simple prayer such as, "Father, I'm a sinner. Please forgive me. I want to live for you," is all that He is seeking.

After accepting Christ as our Lord and Savior, how do we stay faithful and seek Him? We do this by prayer and petition, Bible study and quiet time, and fellowship with other believers.

Wise men and women seek the Lord, but know He is seeking us long before we even know Him. He was seeking us to be His, and spend eternity with Him, in a most wonderful way, over 2,000 years ago, on that first Christmas.

~ Diana Leagh Matthews

Christmas Blessings

My husband and I pastored a church on the northern California coast consisting of a small group of mostly elderly couples and just a few children. Although small, the church provided us with a lovely home plus utilities. However, because of the size and age of our congregation, that was all they could provide. Employment was scarce in the area so our only other income was from my small Avon route.

This was our first Christmas with this church and we were working hard to get the season's activities planned and organized.

As Christmas neared, the large evergreen tree that we had cut stood like a silent sentinel in our front room by the large picture window. Bare of ornaments, it looked forlorn and neglected. We had been so busy planning church activities for our small congregation, that we had not had time to decorate our Christmas tree.

Our son, Clint who was nine, and our daughter, Bethany, five, kept asking us when we were going to get the decorations out of storage and enjoy an evening of family fun decorating our tree. We kept putting them off and it was getting closer and closer to Christmas.

We also realized that we would not have money to get Christmas presents for our children. Grandparents were far away and would send little gifts but we knew it would be a sparse Christmas for us all.

"Mommy, come on, let's decorate the tree," my daughter pleaded one day.

"Soon," I replied.

I began to contemplate: When would we have time to get everything done by Christmas? We had made time to go out into the nearby forest and cut the tree but that seemed like such a long time ago. Where had the days gone?

Finally, setting other tasks aside we decided that we needed to spend the time with our children and get the tree decorated. As the wind whistled and the rain pelted the outside of the windows, we hung strings of lights and our meager supply of decorations. Our children were thrilled when my husband plugged in the lights, then made a fire in our fireplace and we shared a rare moment together as a family.

As Christmas approached, our children again asked when we would have presents to put under our tree. I told them I didn't know and tried to explain to not expect a lot this year. It hurt me to realize our children would not be as fortunate as their friends.

The days passed and our Christmas program began to take shape. The children in our church were excited about the program and we spent many hours preparing costumes and all those things that go into producing a children's program. I had had some experience with working in children's ministry in other churches and gathered previous materials to cut down costs. We realized that there were many children in this community who had never attended church before and we were hoping that by including them in our production they would feel a part of our church.

The Sunday before Christmas finally arrived and our program was a holiday highlight. Parents attended that had never come to our church before and seemed to enjoy the activity. As the day wore down, I realized that there was no mention of a gift for us, the pastor and his family.

Looking around at our church family, I saw the love they had for us. They had showed love in many ways by helping out with groceries and doing kind things for us, but I knew because of their limited incomes, we could expect nothing in the way of presents. Although I had not expected anything, I was hoping at least a card could be passed around and signed with their love. I went home feeling depressed and disappointed and felt as if God was far away.

A few days before Christmas, although our tree looked at home in front of our front window, there were still no presents. Our children were good about not continuing to ask about gifts. I felt proud and humbled when I saw how thrilled they were over small things such as homemade cookies, or helping me out with the other children. But still, we also knew Christmas as we knew it was about presents, however small they might be.

The day before Christmas, I heard a knock at the door and went to see who it was. There stood one of our ladies from the church with gaily wrapped presents in her arms. She came in and set them under our tree. She told me she had saved Green Stamps all year and had purchased gifts for our children, a small doll for our daughter and a game for our son.

She had made a dress and purse for our daughter. She said she could not afford anything else but wanted to give something to our children. Later, another member of our church came by with a gift. She told us she had been working many weeks on an afghan for our family. As she laid her gift under our tree, I felt overwhelmed by the love these dear people felt for us.

Later that day we had another unexpected visitor. A pastor from a distant church came by with a large grocery shower. Bags and bags of groceries were piled on our table. He said that his church had "adopted" us for Christmas and knew we needed food more than gifts. However, he had some small gifts for our children. One lady had purchased a small doll for our daughter and then hand knitted a whole wardrobe for the doll. For our son they purchased a baseball and some other small toys.

On Christmas Eve I noticed another gift under the tree with my name on it. It was from my husband. How had he managed to find the money for a gift for me? He told me he had found a $10 bill on the sidewalk and felt it was God's way of giving me a special Christmas surprise.

On Christmas morning, as we unwrapped the lovely treasures that had been given us, I saw the delight in our children's eyes as they unwrapped gift after gift. I realized that during that busy time when I was so preoccupied with programs and our own church plans, there were those whom God had used to show us true Christmas blessings.

~ Beverly Hill McKinney

The Heart's Desire

Although I'm a grown man, when Christmas rolls around, I remember that special one. I was seven years old, and what I wanted most in the world for Christmas was a BB gun. I asked my parents for it, I prayed for it, and even thought of writing a letter to Santa, but I decided that since I prayed and God had the most power, I'd leave it up to him to tell Santa.

Well, by that time I was a little skeptical about the Santa part, but not the God part. I'd given my life to Jesus the year before.

I knew that was the best thing I could do, but I also knew the "being a good boy for Santa" didn't work with God. You didn't do that for presents. Begging him for a BB gun seemed shallow compared to his already giving me Jesus in my heart.

Since I already had Jesus, the desire of my heart was a BB gun. It was on my mind all during Christmas Eve at church, even as I played the part of a shepherd, and later at home when we gathered to hear Mom read about the birth of Jesus from the Bible. I guess she and Dad knew, that with four children underfoot, we wouldn't listen on Christmas morning.

All night I rolled and turned and dozed and hoped and wanted and anticipated since I'd said "BB Gun" three million, seventeen hundred forty-seven times before Christmas. Didn't want anything else.

Well, finally, I heard movement and saw a shred of light peeking through the window blinds. I whispered, "You awake?" My younger sister jerked upright, blinked, and said, "Yeah," as she moved to the side of her bed.

By the time we got to the next bedroom, our older sisters' feet were hitting the floor. "It's Christmas!" I said as we all ran to the living room.

The Santa piles were always in separate places. The girls found their piles quickly. I moved slowly to mine on the floor in front of the rocking chair because I didn't see anything that looked like a BB Gun.

I didn't care about the unwrapped or the wrapped presents and then my eyes lit on the box in the middle of the rocking chair cushion. It wasn't wrapped and it said BB's on it. I picked it up. It was the biggest box of BB's I'd ever seen. It was heavy. I knew what they'd look like. All shiny and round and little and cool and enough that I could shoot…forever.

But…where was the gun?

Maybe it was an instant but it seemed like eternity that I stood there, clutching that box of BB's, feeling like my world had ended, or maybe had never started, and at the same time reasoning things out.

My thoughts weren't organized but my mind knew things. I was a thinker and my parents taught us about money having to be worked for. We had our regular chores that we didn't get paid for. But Mom also had a list of odd jobs and how much each was worth. We could choose to do any at any time and make a nickel, dime, quarter, and a chore like raking leaves would pay a dollar.

I didn't have time to think it, but it was in me that maybe they thought the BB's would be an incentive to do more jobs, earn the money, and buy my own BB Gun. But that wouldn't be the same as it being my big Christmas Santa gift.

I knew too that I couldn't always have what I asked for. There were four children in our family and one or two, well… three or four… were always wanting or needing something. And we were always being told we couldn't have everything we wanted. Our needs came before our wants. If one got a new pair of shoes, another might have to wait until another paycheck.

Mom had decided not to work outside the home until all of us were in school. My younger sister was three years younger than I and hadn't started kindergarten yet, so our family had only my father's income.

Remember, I was only seven years old. My brain knew all that, even as I stood there kind of numb. But I still had a heart's desire.

Dad's voice said, "Son, look in the corner."

The big Christmas tree was in the corner. My eyes were stuck on the BB box and my hands stiff from squeezing it, but I made my eyes turn to the left and look at the Christmas tree. A few packages were under it, but none the shape of, or long enough to be a BB Gun.

Didn't they know I'd rather have only the BB Gun instead of a lot of presents? But I also knew some would be clothes, and I guessed I always needed those.

"The corner behind the rocking chair, Son."

My gaze moved around, landed on the rocking chair, then went about two feet further and into the corner. I yelled, dropped the box of BB's. There in the corner, leaning against the wall was the most beautiful thing I'd ever seen. My BB Gun!

I held it. And I hugged it. Then I hugged my dad, and my mom. My sisters didn't want to be hugged, so I hugged my gun again, then began the pick-up. (Ever tried to pick up a few thousand BB's? It was a pleasure!)

I don't know if I've ever wanted a present as much as I wanted that gun. A couple of my friends had asked for one too, and got it. We shared with other neighborhood boys. We were more faithful to our shooting than the mailman who had the logo on the side of his vehicle "delivered in rain, hail, sleet, or snow."

Weather didn't matter. We shot cans, lined up objects on fences or boxes and blasted them off, killed plastic and ceramic images, shot each other, and we shot... (Never mind. Mom will read this.)

The fun, fellowship, and playing turned out to be a lengthy, happy time in my life. Looking back I can see it was more than childhood fun, such as being careful because BB shots hurt, becoming proficient in aim, challenge, competing, and accomplishment. The inanimate objects were of no use to anyone, but we did have to do the cleanup (and bury some).

Now that a few decades have passed and I've been a pastor and a teacher, I think of that longing when I was seven, and I contemplate the longings we have in life. Now, as a mature man, I look back to when I was a growing boy, a teenager, a young man, and see how the desires of my heart dominated, changed, were temporary, rolled away like BB's across a hardwood floor. Many desires were fulfilling, others wrong and I'd just like to forget some of them. But I know where the graves are.

We often think of the "if's." If we get our heart's desire, we'll be happy, fulfilled, and worthy. Whether they are good and fulfilling, or used in a wrong way, they're all temporary.

There is still ourselves to face. And eternity.

If we're going to shoot right…forever, then we need to let God be first in our lives.

Without him, all the BB's are useless and temporary, no matter how pretty, how smooth, how cool.

~ David A. Lehman

Mary's Lullaby

In the stillness of the stable
Mary sang a lullaby
As she gently rocked her baby
Neath the starry, winter sky

You're the Word of God Incarnate
You are prophecy fulfilled
You're the Light that shines in darkness
You're the Love of God revealed

You are Alpha and Omega
The Beginning and The End
You're the Hope of all the hopeless
You're the Whisper in the wind

You're the Star from Jacob shining
Holy One of Israel
You're the Servant of Jehovah
You're the Truth within the Veil

You're the Lamb of God, Messiah
You are God's beloved Son
Holy Spirit, God the Father
Ever Three and Ever One

As the shepherds gathered 'round them
And the angel choirs did sing
Mary rocked her little baby
Prince of Peace, and King of Kings

~ *Debra DuPree Williams*

The Best Christmas Present Ever

In 1949, the 21 children in my fifth grade class learned one of life's greatest lessons. Ten-year-olds usually care more about the importance of receiving gifts than considering the joy in giving them. But that year, we found out that giving truly is better than receiving, and it was all because of a special teacher.

Lyle Biddinger served on a navy destroyer during World War II, went to college on the GI Bill and landed in a Chicago suburban grade school teaching fifth grade. We were his first class, and he was the first male teacher in our kindergarten through eighth grade school. Young, handsome, and an outstanding teacher, he was all any 10-year-old could ask for.

During family dinners, I talked about what "Mr. Bid" had told us that day, what he'd shown us, the games he'd taught us. He might as well have been sitting at our table every night, for his presence was evident Monday through Friday. I hurried through breakfast so I could get to school early, and I offered to stay after class and do whatever little jobs needed to be done. I wasn't the only one who acted this way about Mr. Biddinger. Oh no — all of us adored him.

We were so proud to be in his class. We strutted like peacocks displaying their feathers around the kids in the other fifth grade class. He was all ours, and like kids of that age, we let everyone know it. Mr. Biddinger made learning fun — and in the 1940's this was a new approach. At one point, some of the parents went to the principal and complained that he spent too much time playing games during class time; school should not be fun, but hard work. Somehow Mr. Biddinger and the principal placated the disgruntled parents, and life went on as before.

December arrived, and the Room Mother contacted the other parents. Each family was asked to give a modest amount of money to be used for a Christmas gift for the teacher. It was not an unusual request in our school. Next she called Mr. Biddinger's wife to find out what might be the perfect gift for him.

It was to be a secret, but we all knew about it, and whispers and notes flew back and forth. Our class Christmas party would be held the last day before the holiday break. We would have punch, cookies, candy, and a grab bag gift exchange. We'd play some games, get out of schoolwork and give Mr. Bid his gift. The days trickled by slower than ever before, and our excitement grew steadily. We looked forward to our school Christmas much more than the one we'd each have at home.

Finally, the big day dawned. Our Room Mother arrived bearing the punch and brightly decorated Christmas cookies and hard candies. But where was the big box Mr. Bid's present was in? We didn't see it. We wriggled in our desks and fretted. Whispers sailed around the room until Mr. Bid scolded us.

"Settle down," he said, "or the party's over as of now."

Quiet reigned. The treats and grab bag gifts were passed out. We munched on our sugar cookies and slurped the red punch. The classroom door opened, and a strange woman walked in. Mr. Biddinger looked surprised, then a big smile crossed his face. He introduced his wife. The Room Mother disappeared into the hall but was back in seconds holding a good-sized box wrapped in Christmas paper and tied with a wide red ribbon. The chatter in the room ceased immediately, and all eyes were riveted on that box.

The Room Mother cleared her throat, walked to our teacher and said, "Mr. Biddinger, this gift is from your students. They wanted to show their love and appreciation by giving you something special." As she handed him the box, the room tingled with an air of excitement.

Mr. Bid seemed excited, and that thrilled us. He untied the bow and handed the ribbon to his wife. Next came the wrapping. We all leaned forward. He opened the box and lifted a hunting jacket from the folds of tissue paper. Mrs. Biddinger had told the Room Mother that was his fondest wish for Christmas. He loved to hunt on the weekends whenever possible, but special hunting gear was beyond a teacher's salary.

For the first time, the man who taught us so much became speechless. He turned the jacket over and over, looked at the special pockets on the inside and outside. He tried again to say something but couldn't. But the sparkle in his eyes and the smile on his face said all we needed to know.

He finally found his voice and told us over and over how much he loved his new jacket. "It's probably the finest gift I've ever received," he said. He didn't say why, but we knew. We had no doubt that the reason was that it came from his first class, the 21 10-year-olds who adored him.

I don't remember the gifts I received at home that Christmas, but I'll never forget the gift we gave Mr. Biddinger. It was the best Christmas present ever.

~ Nancy Julien Kopp

Butterfly Tree

If anyone is in Christ, he is a new creation;
old things have passed away;
behold all things have become new.
2 Corinthians 5:17 KJV

While attending a nature seminar I listened to an expert talk about his love of butterflies. He raises these winged jewels and sells them for special occasions such as weddings, funerals and other memorable events. Some of his butterflies have even appeared in movies.

I was especially struck with his story about how he decorated his Christmas tree one year. He told of how he refrigerated a large number of chrysalides to slow down the process of metamorphosis. As he decorated his tree with them he lowered the thermostat in the room. Rising before his family in the wee hours of Christmas morning, he raised the thermostat to just the right temperature required to have the butterflies hatch at a precise time. When his family came downstairs the tree was alive with brilliantly colored butterflies gently fanning their wings to dry. What a gorgeous sight to behold!

Like the butterfly that must leave behind the ugly cocoon to soar on its beautiful wings, when we receive the Lord's gift of salvation, we exchange our old self with its burden of sin and gladly put on the new self that is beautifully clothed in His righteousness.

As I reflected on the poignancy of the moment when I became a new creature in Christ, leaving behind my old self while reveling in the freedom I had found through His forgiveness, I thanked the Lord for the wonderful gift of His Son, Jesus.

Dearest Lord, thank You for providing the way for us to leave our old self behind and be made new in You. Amen.

~ *Bonnie Mae Evans*

The Christmas Cave

Sunlight gleams on my olivewood nativity set from Bethlehem. Carved figures of the Holy family cluster under the wooden roof. Shepherds with their sheep kneel in front of the stable while wise men stand nearby.

Similar scenes around the world commemorate Jesus's birth.

It reminds me of my trip to Israel and the visit to Bethlehem. At the Church of the Nativity, built over the traditional site of Jesus's birth, and constructed centuries after Jesus was born, the low doorway forced visitors to duck at the entry of the dim church. A line of hundreds of tourists curved along the stone walls. Although everyone in our tour group hoped to see the place of his birth, a two-hour wait prompted us to change our plans.

After conferring with our guide, we decided to visit another cave located under St. Catherine's Catholic Church. Many believe this could be the cave where Jesus was born. We descended a narrow, stone staircase and entered a less crowded area. Our group filled a small, simple cave.

No one spoke for several minutes. Then our voices blended into a melodious choir as we sang "Silent Night." Peace enveloped the room and caressed my heart.

Although our initial itinerary changed, God provided a more serene place to experience and worship him. No one lined up behind us or hurried us along.

Which cave was the "real" one?

I didn't know nor did it matter. Scripture records Jesus's birthplace as being in Bethlehem. Therefore, just being in the city and experiencing the peace of God with other believers made the visit meaningful. Incredible memories of that unexpected visit remain.

Instead, when circumstances alter carefully crafted plans, Jesus meets us with his superior ones. Instead of "seeing" a cave, we were able to worship and experience the wonder of what occurred in a stable-cave in Bethlehem.

My olivewood nativity set reminds me of that life-changing trip to the Holy Land, and more importantly, the significance of Jesus's birth. I may not be sure in which cave he was born, but I know which heart has been reborn. Mine.

Rebirth is available to all who will accept it. We can experience that Christmas Spirit now, and forever.

~ Rebecca Carpenter

67

Christmas Lives On

T hose of us who have accepted Jesus and surrendered our lives to him celebrate the real meaning of Christmas throughout the year. We know the reality of it, even in stressful times when we can't feel the joy.

We save the decorating, gift buying, commercialism, until November and December...well, maybe not. We hear about those Christmases in July, other months, and even April, as I mentioned in the introduction about watching *The Star of Bethlehem*.

Below is a list of authors and their books that include Christmas in some way. You might want to read these and enjoy the entertainment and real meaning of Christmas all year long.

~ Yvonne Lehman

Novels

Carole Brown
Sabotaged Christmas

Melody Carlson, one adult novella each year
The Christmas Angels' Project
The Christmas Joy Ride
The Christmas Cat
A Simple Christmas Wish
The Christmas Pony
The Christmas Shoppe
Christmas at Harrington'
The Christmas Dog
The Joy of Christmas
The Treasure of Christmas
An Irish Christmas
The Christmas Bus
All I Have to Give
The Gift of Christmas Present

Lori Copeland
Beautiful Star of Bethlehem
Unwrapping Christmas
Christmas Vows: $5.00 Extra
The Christmas Lamp

Susan Page Davis, novellas included in
Mountain Christmas Brides
The 12 Brides of Christmas

Louise Gouge
Cowgirl Under the Mistletoe
Yuletide Reunion (in *A Western Christmas anthology*)

Sandra Merville Hart
A Stranger On My Land

Yvonne Lehman
Crashing into Love
Let It Snow
Better Latte than Never

Elizabeth Ludwig
Christmas Comes to Bethlehem, Maine

Vickie McDonough
The Christmas Brides Collection
The 12 Brides of Christmas Collection
Wild West Christmas
Christmas Mail-Order Brides

Lori Roeleveld
Red Pen Redemption

Linda Rondeau
A Christmas Prayer (aka *A Father's Prayer*)
A Wonderful Love (formerly *It Really IS a Wonderful Life*)
Miracle on Maple Street

Becky Wade, (short story available for download on Amazon)
The Proposal

Dan Walsh
Keeping Christmas
Remembering Christmas
The Unfinished Gift

Stephanie Grace Whitson, Judith McCoy Miller, and Nancy Moser and
Stephanie Grace Whitson, two novella anthologies
A Patchwork Christmas
A Basket Brigade Christmas

Non-fiction Compilations (Multiple Authors)

Christmas Moments
More Christmas Moments
Additional Christmas Moments

About the Authors

Cathy Ancewicz was born and raised in New Hampshire near the shores of Lake Winnipesaukee. She spent 22 years on the north shore of Long Island, New York, where she and her husband, Edward, raised their only child, Heidi. She has now settled on the east coast of south Florida. Catherine spent many years in the art field honing her craft in calligraphy, and has taught the beautiful script to groups of artists. Writing is her new passion. She joined her church's Creative Writing Ministry in 2013 where she learned to write short stories and novels. Her story, "A Hero's Welcome" is published in *Chicken Soup for the Soul — The Spirit of America*. She is writing a novel and stories about her childhood adventures.

Carolyn Roth Barnum moved from Michigan to Kentucky in 2012. She and her husband, Clair Barnum, were married 59 years before his death in 2009. This is her second published writing. Her first story, "Can't Live Here Any More," appeared in *Precious, Precocious Moments*. She is featured in *The Write Life*'s May 2016 Subscriber Spotlight. During her career she held various secretarial and executive assistant positions including planning and coordinating state and international conferences for the Michigan District of Kiwanis. She is coordinator for Write People, a writer's group in Wesley Village. She enjoys writing, reading, involvement in various activities at Wesley Village, and spending time with family and friends.

Robin Bayne is an award-winning author of 17 novels, novellas and short stories. She compiled a collection of devotions for writers titled *Words to Write By*. She lives in Maryland with her husband of 25 years. Visit her website, *Robin Bayne*, at rbayne.com.

Debby Bellingham (DMin, Christian Spiritual Formation) is a Spiritual Director, licensed psychotherapist, ordained minister, author and experienced retreat facilitator. She lives in New York with her husband, Jack, and her pugs, Molly and Ellie. She enjoys learning new things, running, and hanging out with her grandchildren. You can learn more about her by visiting her at *TheMentoredLife.com*.

Charlotte Burkholder enjoys writing devotionals and personal experience stories. Many of her devotionals have been published by *The Secret Place*. Other writings have appeared in *Celebrate Life, Women Alive, Evangel, The Gem, The Family Digest,* and *Christian Communicator*. Her stories have also been published in *Stories of God's Abundance, Why Fret the God Stuff,* and *"Help Lord, I'm Having a Senior Moment."* Charlotte lives in Virginia with her husband, Marlin. They have been married for 56 years. Their four children and spouses have blessed them with 12 wonderful grandchildren.

Janet Bryant Campbell is a free-lance writer and playwright. Her favorite plays are those co-written with her son, Nathan Campbell. They include *Locked Away, All That Glitters,* the outdoor drama *Martyrs and Mayhem,* and a dinner theater production, *Mystery at the Manger*. Janet, a dog lover, is owned by a six-pound Pomeranian. After her Pomeranian was diagnosed with the autoimmune disease, Immune Mediated Hemolytic Anemia, or IMHA, in 2013, Janet has focused on writing articles that help other pet owners deal with this disease and to raise awareness among pet owners. Janet is currently working on turning stories she wrote for her son as a child into a series of children's picture books. She is also diving into her favorite genre, and has started work on a mystery novel.

LeAnn Campbell is married to Bud. They have six adult children and numerous grandchildren and great-grandchildren. LeAnn resumed her college education at age 40 and is a retired special education teacher. Her published works include over 1,600 articles and stories, two devotional books, and the *Century Farm* series of mysteries for middle-grade readers. Visit her blog, *Preserving Family Memories*, at leanncampbell.com.

Rebecca Carpenter writes at her lake retreat in Florida. After retiring from teaching elementary school, she and her husband traveled the world for missions and pleasure. Experiences with her granddaughters, traveling, and nature inspire her writings. Her articles have appeared in *Adventures in Odyssey Clubhouse* magazine, *Posh Parenting, Christmas Moments, Celebrating Christmas with...Memories, Poetry, and Good Food,* and several local publications. After losing her husband and both parents within months, she wrote page after page of her grief journey. Forty of those devotionals are available in her book *Ambushed by Glory*. Visit her blog, *Inspirations from Life,* at rebeccacarpenter.blogspot.com.

Autumn J. Conley became a full-time freelance book editor in 2009, but writing has been her lifelong passion, ever since she was first published in the local paper at age 14. She has penned many essays, op-ed pieces, short stories, poems, and articles, as well as two books, a single-parenting column, and, most recently, a featured weight-loss blog for *Sparkpeople.com*. She has won many local and international writing contests, and her work is published in *Chicken Soup for the Mothers of Preschooler's Soul, Soul Matters for Moms, The Bad Hair Day Book,* and magazines such as *Home Life, All You, Jr. Trails, New Moon for Girls, Kansas Child,* and *Primary Treasures.* In addition to writing and editing, Autumn busies herself with geocaching, a hobby she enjoys in the great outdoors with family and friends. She lives in Ohio with her daughter, Cissy, and three small dogs. Visit her on Facebook.

Maresa DePuy has a B.A. in Journalism from Indiana University and has worked in non-profit public relations for the American Red Cross and United Cerebral Palsy Associations. She travels throughout Uganda interacting with people living in poverty and those who have been lifted out of it by Hands of Love. Through her experiences in Uganda, Maresa has developed a valuable perspective through which she sees the enormous chasm, yet often startling similarities, between following Christ in the First and Third Worlds. She blogs at *PebbleThrowers.org* and resides in South Carolina where she lives on mission as a wife to one and mom to two.

Sharon Blackstock Dobbs has been sharing her poetry and prose with family and friends for five decades. Sharon downsized her home but not her life. She wants to share her poetry and prose with a larger following. Sending her words into the world just as she has her two sons, she prays that they will be an encouragement to others.

Susan Dollyhigh is a freelance writer and speaker. She is a contributing author in *Spirit and Heart: A Devotional Journey; Faith and Finances: In God We Trust; The Ultimate Christian Living; God Still Meets Needs,* and *I Believe in Heaven.* Susan's articles have appeared in *Connection Magazine, Exemplify Magazine, Mustard Seed Ministry, P31 Woman, The Upper Room,* and *The Secret Place.*

Kristin Dossett lives in Kentucky with her husband of seven years and their three young boys. She has a Master of Science in Nursing from Vanderbilt University and works as a nurse practitioner in a pediatric primary care clinic. She blogs at *LoveMercyWalkHumbly.com.*

Terri Elders received her first byline in 1946 on a piece about how bats saved her family's home from fire, published on the children's page of the *Portland Oregonian.* At nine years of age, she hadn't known that her title, "Bats in Our Belfry," would lead readers to suspect her family's sanity. Her stories have appeared in over 100 anthologies. Visit her at *ATouchofTarragon.blogspot.com.*

Susan Engebrecht has written for a variety of magazines, *Chicken Soup for the Soul,* Lighthouse Publishing of the Carolinas, and worked as a columnist. She has won a number of writing and speaking awards; judges writing and speaking contests; served on the board for Wisconsin Writers Association, and is currently co-director for the Green Lake Christian Writers Conference held each year in August. Her husband, aka in her writings as Knight-in-faded-blue-jeans, a bossy puggle, and five take-your-breath-away-brilliant grandchildren provide endless joy and writing material.

Bonnie Mae Evans is a Registered Nurse, mom and writer. One of her greatest joys is sharing the love of God through the written word. As a member of Mountain Christian Church Writer's Group she contributes regularly to their devotional blog. Several of her devotions and short stories have been published in five books. She has also written a Christian novel.

Dorothy Floyd has made her home in Georgia for over 20 years. She finds life as a single mom and a special education teacher both challenging and rewarding. In the next few years, Dorothy plans to retire from teaching, and publish her collection of devotional stories taken from life experiences.

Gayle Fraser has two children, five grandchildren, seven great-grandchildren. After working 35 years as an Administrative Secretary in Arizona, she retired and began writing seriously. She belongs to Wordy Ones, a local writers group, and Word Weavers International. She has self-published a girls' curriculum, *Dove,* and *Grandma's Faithfulness Prayer Warriors* for Christian grandmothers. Her program, *Shush, I'm a Secret Sister,* for women wanting to be a secret sister of a pre-teen has been used successfully in several churches. She has self-published a book for children, and *Love Stories from Grandma's Heart* for her grandchildren. She and her husband smuggled Bibles into China, participated in the Billy Graham Crusade in Moscow, Russia, toured Israel, and took their granddaughter to Hungary with their church's youth group. Two of her stories are published in *Additional Christmas Moments.*

Janice S. Garey lives in Georgia with husband Art, and Miss Bosley, a stray kitten who arrived in a divine moment for Christmas 2013. Janice's publishing credits include book reviews, an article in *Church Libraries*, and an article in the *Christian Library International* (CLI) newsletter about the need for Spanish language Bibles in prisons. As a CLI volunteer she hopes to reach prisoners and the world with God's word. She volunteers in the church media center and treasures Women's Missionary Union relationships. She has taken writing courses with Christian Writers Guild.

Tommy Scott Gilmore, III, a gifted speaker and motivational leader, is Executive Director of Changing Lives Ministry in Asheville, North Carolina. His life has not been boring. To experience poverty, he spent a winter's month in Boston's ghetto with only 50¢ in his pocket. He rode a bicycle over 20,000 miles through 20 states and 12 countries, climbed St. Goddard Pass in the Swiss Alps and cheated death on several occasions by surviving quicksand, numerous auto accidents and threats on his life from his preaching. He is happily married to Sandra Gault Gilmore formerly of South Carolina. They have three grown daughters, Lindsey, Brittany and Meghan, and two grandchildren, Sarah Grace and Victoria. You can find his life-changing testimony on his website: *ChangingLivesMinistry.info*.

Jean Matthew Hall lives in beautiful North Carolina. Her stories and articles have appeared in a variety of inspirational magazines and anthologies. Her life's mission is to teach, nurture and encourage others. Visit Jean at *JeanMatthewHall.com*, and on Facebook and Twitter.

Kristen Harmon lives in Florida with her husband, Joe. She works in Human Resources and enjoys writing stories and blogging at *Full of Grace:* tuesdayschildren.blogspot.com.

Kay Harper spent her childhood exploring, her 20s rebelling, 30s on a quest, 40s in Never-Never Land and 50s lost and found. Through it all her pen has been a trusted companion. Kay has published several of her award-winning short stories online and the old fashioned way. She writes from her home in Florida, minutes from the white-sand beaches of the Gulf of Mexico.

Lydia E. Harris has been married to her college sweetheart, Milt, for 48 years. They have two married children and five grandchildren ranging from preschool to high school. Lydia earned a Master of Arts degree in home economics. She has written numerous articles, book reviews, devotionals, and stories. *Clubhouse* magazine for children publishes her recipes, which she develops and tests with her grandchildren. She writes the column "A Cup of Tea with Lydia," and is called "Grandma Tea" by her grandchildren. Lydia has contributed to numerous books and is author of the book, *Preparing My Heart for Grandparenting: For Grandparents at Any Stage of the Journey*.

Lori Hatcher is the author of the five-minute devotional, *Hungry for God...Starving for Time*. The editor of *Reach Out, Columbia* magazine, Lori's passion is to help busy women connect to God in the craziness of everyday life. An award-winning Toastmasters International speaker, she shares five-minute words of encouragement on her blog, *Hungry for God*, at lorihatcher.com

Karen R. Hessen's writings have been published in six volumes of *Chicken Soup for the Soul; Guideposts; When God Makes Lemonade; RAIN Magazine 2013, 2014, 2015* and *2016; Preciou,s Precocious Moments;* and *More Christmas Moments.* Her work also appears in *Vista* (12 times); *The Secret Place* (eight times); *The Mother's Heart Magazine; Help! I'm A Parent; God Makes Lemonade; CAP Connection; Apple Hill Cider Press; Seeds of... A Collection of Writings by Pacific Northwest Authors,* and others. The release of *Jesus Encounters* includes her latest published work. "My Best Name" was previously published in *The Mother's Heart,* a small e-zine targeting homeschooling parents.

Helen L. Hoover enjoys sewing, reading, knitting, and traveling. She and her husband are retired, live in Northwest Arkansas and volunteer at a Christian college. They are blessed with two grown children, four grandchildren and four great-grandchildren. Helen's devotions and personal stories are published in books and Christian handout papers.

Terri Kelly is the author of *Mary Slessor: Missionary Mother.* As a writer she has contributed to several books, including *Divine Moments, Faith and Family,* and *Spirit and Heart.* Terri has published articles in *The Kids' Ark* magazine, *Clubhouse, WHOA Magazine,* and numerous online publications. Her blog, *TerriBKelly.com,* addresses issues teachers deal with on a daily basis. She teaches at writing conferences and assists with the Asheville Christian Writers Conference in North Carolina.

Nancy Julien Kopp, originally from Chicago, has lived in the Kansas Flint Hills for many years. She writes creative nonfiction, memoir, inspirational, award winning children's fiction, poetry and articles on the writing craft. She's published in 18 *Chicken Soup for the Soul* books, other anthologies, newspapers, e-zines and Internet radio. She blogs about her writing world with tips and encouragement for writers at *WriterGrannysWorld.blogspot.com.*

Luke Lehman is grandson of Yvonne Lehman, compiler of the *Moments* series. He wrote his article, about his most memorable Christmas, as an assignment when he shadowed Yvonne as part of his high school senior project. Luke lives with his family in North Carolina.

David A. Lehman's poem "Today It Rained Gorillas," written when he was seven years old, and his short story, "The Accident," written when he was nine years old, are published in *Precious Precocious Moments.* In *Additional Christmas Moments,* he writes about his most memorable childhood Christmas, which occurred when he was seven years old. David is an author of technical writing. He is a pastor and educator, has three children, and lives in North Carolina.

Yvonne Lehman is author of 57 novels. She founded, and directed for 25 years, the Blue Ridge Mountains Christian Writers Conference. She now directs the Blue Ridge Novelist Retreat held annually in October at Ridgecrest Conference Center in North Carolina. She lives in North Carolina with her beautiful furry blond and white Pomeranian, Rigel, named after a Titanic survivor. In addition to the *Moments* series, her latest books include a novella, *Have Dress Will Marry,* in the *Heart of a Cowboy* collection; and a compilation, *Writing Right to Success,* by 25 authors about their journey to success and craft articles for writers; and a cozy mystery, *Better Latte than Never.* Her popular 50th book is *Hearts that Survive — A Novel of the Titanic,* which she signs periodically at the Titanic Museum in Pigeon Forge, Tennessee.

Diana Leagh Matthews is a vocalist, speaker, writer, life coach, and genealogist. She is a Christian Communicators and Christian Devotions Boot Camp graduate. She has been published in several anthologies, including *Spoken Moments* and *More Christmas Moments.* She currently resides in South Carolina. Visit her website, *DianaLeaghMatthews.com,* and her blog, *ALookThruTime.com.*

Beverly Hill McKinney has published over 300 inspirational articles in such publications as *Good Old Days, Breakthrough Intercessor, Just Between Us, Women Alive, P31,* and *Plus Magazine.* She has devotions in *Cup of Comfort Devotional: Daily Reflections of God's Love and Grace, Open Windows, God Still Meets Needs,* and *God Still Leads and Guides.* Her stories have been featured in anthologies such as *Christmas Miracles, Men of Honor,* Guidepost's *Extraordinary Answers to Prayer, Christian Miracles,* and *Precious, Precocious Moments.* She has also self-published two books, *Through the Parsonage Window* and *Whispers from God: Poems of Inspiration.* She graduated from the Jerry B. Jenkins Christian Writer's Guild and lives in Oregon.

Mary E. McQueen has served for many years as an ordained minister. She has lived in many states and completed studies in Europe. She and her husband Ken (also ordained) live and serve churches in Lincoln, Nebraska. They have five grown children. Mary has served as a police chaplain and is a facilitator in the Anti Violence Project inside prison walls. She and her husband are childbirth and gentle parenting instructors and she has coached and helped deliver a large number of healthy babies as part of her ministry. Her story "A Dog, A Broken Boy and a Beer Truck" is about an actual event.

Norma C. Mezoe has been a published writer for 30 years. Her writing has appeared in books, devotionals, take-home papers and magazines. She lives in a tiny town in Indiana where she is active in her church as clerk, teacher and bulletin maker.

Julie Miller has been inspiring children, youth, and women as a speaker, teacher, quiet day retreat leader, author and mentor for over 30 years. She was the Director of Women's Bible Studies at Eagle Brook Church; is a certified Spiritual Director; and owns Heart Matters Publishing Company. She is an alumnus of Bethel University and Christos Center for Spiritual Formation. She has written Bible Study curriculum and devotionals, including the collaboration, *Whispers of God's Grace: Stories to Encourage Your Heart.* Julie draws on her wide range of life experiences, humor, and love of God's Word and His creation for her writing. When she is not writing, you will find her absorbed in a good book, puttering in her garden or dreaming of France. Julie and her husband, Rey, live in Minnesota and are the parents of two grown sons, Erik and Kyle.

Lynn Mosher has a deep passion to share her devotionals and inspirational stories, fulfilling God's call on her life to encourage others and glorify the Lord. She is published in the books: *Entering the God of Wholeness, Ya Know What I'm Say'n,* and *Overwhelmed: 31 Stories from M.O.M.* She contributes to sites and magazines, including *Secret Place, Comfort Café, Internet Café, Novel Rocket, High Calling, CrossReads,* and *AuthorCulture.* Lynn is a monthly columnist for online and print venues including: *TheMOMInitiative.com, LivingBetterat50+, Ruby for Women, Daily Signs of Hope, Lift Up Your Day for Women, The Consilium* and *Grace&Faith4U.* Her first book is in the process of being published and she is working on her second book. She also writes twice weekly on her own website *LynnMosher.com.*

Vicki H. Moss is Contributing Editor and past Editor-at-Large for *Southern Writers Magazine.* A columnist for the *American Daily Herald,* she's also a poet, a Precept Ministries Leader, a Christian Communicators graduate, and author of *How to Write for Kids' Magazines* and *Writing with Voice.* She has written for *Hopscotch* and *Boy's Quest* magazines for the last decade in addition to being published in *Christmas Moments, Divine Moments* and *Precious, Precocious Moments,* SouthWest Writer's *SouthWest Sage, Country Woman, In the City, Borderlines,* Scotland's *Thistle Blower,* and *I Believe in Heaven.* She was selected to be a presenter of her fiction and creative nonfiction short stories for three consecutive Southern Women Writers Conferences. Vicki is a speaker and faculty member for writers conferences. She is also a photographer who does book styling to help authors promote novels, poetry, and non-fiction. For more information visit her online at *LivingWaterFiction.com.*

Marilyn Nutter of South Carolina is the author of three devotional books and a contributor to on-line sites, compilations and is former editor of *Penned from the Heart.* She is a Bible teacher and speaker for women's community and church groups, a grief support facilitator, and serves on the women's ministry council at her church. Visit her website *Extraordinary Treasures,* at marilynnutter.com.

Dianna Owens is a blogger who reaches out to the community through *Ignite 2 Ignite,* a women's ministry. She is published in *Living Real Magazine, Reach Out Columbia* and *Precious, Precocious Moments.* Dianna is a full-time single mom to an 11-year-old boy and five-year-old daughter. She resides in Lexington, South Carolina. Her journaling about this journey of life can be found at her website *DiannaOwens.com.*

Colleen L. Reece describes herself as an ordinary person with an extraordinary God. Raised in a home without electricity or running water but filled with love for God and family, Colleen learned to read by kerosene lamplight and dreamed of someday writing a book. God has multiplied her "someday" book into *150 Books You Can Trust,* with six million copies sold.

Alisha Ritchie writes from North Carolina where she enjoys spending time with Brandon, her husband of 20 years, and two wonderful teenagers, Zack and Abby. She is a Physical Therapy Assistant and a multi-published author of devotions and stories to inspire others in their walk with God. Alisha's stories and devotions have appeared in *Today's Christian Living* magazine, *Devotions,* multiple websites, and as a contribution to *Mixed Blessings* scheduled for release in 2017. She is ecstatic about her devotional book, *Snuggle Sessions with God.* Alisha is passionate about writing but also enjoys socializing with family and friends, exploring the waterfalls of North Carolina, being an active member of her Baptist church and encouraging women through her community Women's Ministry Group. You can read more of her writing at *ChristianDevotions.us*, *2 Me from Him* at normagail.org, and *Thoughts-About-God.com/blog*.

Robert B. Robeson has been published 875 times in 320 publications in 100 countries. This includes the *Reader's Digest, Positive Living, Vietnam Combat, Official Karate, Frontier Airline Magazine* and *Newsday*, among others. He's also been featured in 45 anthologies. He flew 978 medical evacuation missions in South Vietnam (1969-1970), evacuated over 2,500 patients from both sides of the action, had seven helicopters shot up by enemy fire and was shot down twice in one year. After 19 years as a medevac pilot on three continents, and over 27 years of military service, he retired from the U.S. Army as a lieutenant colonel. After retiring, he served as a newspaper managing editor and columnist. Robeson has a BA in English from the University of Maryland-College Park and has completed extensive undergraduate and graduate work in journalism at the University of Nebraska-Lincoln. He's a life member of the National Writers Association, the VFW, the Distinguished Flying Cross Society and the Dustoff Association. He lives in Nebraska with his wife, Phyllis. They have been married 47 years.

David Russell is semi-retired. He resides with his wife in lower Michigan, and enjoys freelance writing, blogging, playing piano, and moderate exercise. He has published one faith-based novel, and over the past four years has contributed to other anthologies and e-zines. Contact David through his blog, *GraftedInAndOnTheJourney.blogspot.com*.

Toni Armstrong Sample retired from Pennsylvania to South Carolina at the end of a successful career as a Human Resource executive, and owner of a management consulting, training, and development firm. A published author in journals and magazines, in 2014 she celebrated the release of her first three novels of inspiration, intrigue and romance, *The Glass Divider, Transparent Web of Dreams*, and *Distortion*. Toni is a Christian retreat leader, conference speaker, Bible study facilitator, and commission artist.

Beverly Sce, PhD., author, inspirational speaker, founder and director of the Jesus Divine Mercy Ministry has been featured in health care publications and enjoys writing stories that inspire. Her works have appeared in magazines and books including, *Reminisce* and *The Extraordinary Presence of God*. She is a member of the Pearl S. Buck Writers Guild and was published in the inaugural edition of the *Pearl S. Buck Literary Journal*. Beverly has completed the Amherst Writers and Artists Training Program and is certified to use the Amherst Writers and Artists method to lead writing workshops that are "committed to the belief that a writer is someone who writes and that every writer has a unique voice." She has a passion for cooking and baking "from scratch" (which she learned from her mom), enjoys travel, and is an avid reader and quilter who loves hand applique and making Broderie Perse quilts. Born and raised in New Jersey, Beverly and her husband Doug now call beautiful Bucks County, Pennsylvania home. While she holds a PhD in Health Psychology/Behavioral Medicine, she is pursuing her writing goal and completing a MFA in creative non-fiction.

June Schmidt lives in the gorgeous Blue Ridge Mountains in North Carolina. Her article, "Angels Wore Blue Jeans and Drove Pickup Trucks" is published in *Divine Moments*. In 1993 she packed her first Samaritan's Purse Shoe Box, thinking it seemed like a small thing to do. But as years passed, her interest grew and so did the number of shoeboxes. In 2004 she began collecting shoeboxes for her church. Her desire to help children all over the world became her passion. Now she's in charge of the church's shoe boxes — hundreds each year — that get lined up in front of the church where prayers are then offered for the boxes, the children, and Samaritan's Purse.

Annmarie B. Tait resides in Pennsylvania with her husband, Joe Beck. In addition to writing stories about her large Irish Catholic family and the memories they made, she enjoys singing and recording Irish and American folk songs with her husband. Among her other passions are cooking, sewing and crocheting. Annmarie has over 50 stories published in various anthologies including *Chicken Soup for the Soul* and the *Patchwork Path* series.

Donn Taylor led an Infantry rifle platoon in the Korean War, served with Army aviation in Vietnam, and worked with air reconnaissance in Europe and Asia. Afterwards, he earned a PhD in English literature (Renaissance) and for 18 years taught literature at two liberal arts colleges. His poetry has appeared in leading journals and is collected in his book *Dust and Diamond: Poems of Earth and Beyond*. In addition to the historical novel *Lightning on a Quiet Night*, his fiction includes two light-hearted mysteries, *Rhapsody in Red* and *Murder Mezzo Forte*, and two suspense novels, *Deadly Additive* and *The Lazarus File*, which has been re-issued as an e-book. He is a frequent speaker at writers' groups and conferences. He lives near Houston Texas, where he continues to write fiction and poetry, as well as essays on writing, ethical issues, and U.S. foreign policy.

Denise Valuk lives and writes in Texas. She has been married to William for 25 years and they have three sons, Collin, Caleb, and Cooper. In between homeschooling the two younger boys and hiking throughout Texas, Denise enjoys writing for inspirational publications and the kids' ministry program within her local church. Her work is included in *Guideposts Magazine, Mysterious Ways Magazine, Chicken Soup for the Soul: Touched by An Angel,* and *Chicken Soup for the Soul: Think Possible*. Denise can be reached via her website: DeniseValuk.com.

Jen Waldron is first and foremost a child of the King. Born and raised in northern New England, she now resides with her husband of more than 30 years just outside sunny Atlanta. When not working as a registered nurse, she spends time writing and baking, and then baking and writing. Her publications are based on personal memories and the humor in life. She is incredibly thankful for three wonderful sons and three adorable grandsons and the inspiration they provide. Vacations are spent along a multitude of coastlines because secretly she wishes being a sea glass hunter was an actual occupation.

Barbara Wells is the published author of *Steeple People* and *Cameos*, a gift book of poetry, and is contributing author to *I Believe in Heaven* and *I Believe in Healing*. Wells serves on the Executive Board for the Kentucky Christian Writers Conference, is a member of AWSA (Advanced Writers and Speakers Association), and the host of *Steeple People Talk Radio*. For more information, visit her website: barbarawells.webs.com.

Kathy Whirity is a syndicated newspaper columnist who shares her sentimental musings on family life. She is the author of *Life Is a Kaleidoscope*, a compilation of her most popular columns. Visit her website: KathyWhirity.com.

Debra DuPree Williams is a classically trained lyric-coloratura soprano, but her first love is southern Gospel. She began writing when she was a young girl and finished her first novel when she was in the seventh grade. Her essay, *A Tribute to Shan Palmer,* appeared in the online magazine, *Dead Mule School of Southern Literature*. She is a member of SCBWI and ACFW. At the 2015 Autumn in the Mountains Novel Retreat, her unpublished cozy mystery, *Grave Consequences*, won second place for best book proposal. When she isn't busy writing, she can be found chasing an elusive ancestor, either through online sources or in country graveyards. She enjoys painting, quilting, or cooking up something totally southern. She has been married to Jim for 43 years. They are the proud parents of four sons, Ken, Christopher, Adam, and Daniel, one amazing daughter-in-law, Cecili, and two beautiful granddaughters, Piper and Emerson. She and Jim live in North Carolina.

www.ingramcontent.com/pod-product-compliance
Lightning Source LLC
Chambersburg PA
CBHW071434090426
42737CB00011B/1661